TALES OF
ST COLUMBA

A NOTE ON THE AUTHOR

Eileen Dunlop was born and went to school in Alloa, Clackmannanshire, Scotland, near where she now lives. She has published nine novels for children, of which *The House on the Hill* (1987) was commended for the Carnegie Medal, *Finn's Island* (1991) commended for the McVitie's Prize for the Scottish Writer of the Year and *The Maze Stone* (1982) and *Clementina* (1985) won Scottish Arts Council Book Awards. She has also, with her husband, Antony Kamm, written several information books on Scottish themes, and compiled two collections of verse.

TALES OF ST COLUMBA

Eileen Dunlop

POOLBEG

For Derry and Jeanne Jeffares

First published 1992 by
Poolbeg Press Ltd
Knocksedan House,
Swords, Co Dublin, Ireland

© Eileen Dunlop, 1992

The moral right of the author has been asserted.

Poolbeg Press receives assistance from
the Arts Council / An Chomhairle Ealaíon, Ireland.

ISBN 1 85371 134 9

Cover illustration by Carol Betera
Set by Richard Parfrey in Stone Serif 10/14
Printed by Cox and Wyman Ltd Reading Berks

Contents

1

Eithne's Story

Eithne was tired. Even a princess whose baby would soon be born was not encouraged to sit all day doing nothing. She had spent most of the day weaving cloth at her loom, and all of the evening in the great hall, where her husband, Feidhlimí, the chief, was feasting with his friends. They seemed always to be feasting, these large, golden-haired men who loved battles and tales of battles, wine, music, and good company. The old bard Geamán had arrived at Gartan that afternoon, and the men would sit in the hall far into the night, listening to his songs of Cú Chulainn and Oisín and Niamh of the Golden Hair. Even Christians in Erin loved these wonderful tales of long ago.

But Eithne was not hungry, and the intense heat of the low-roofed hall exhausted her. After supper she slipped away, thankful to return to her quiet room. The fire burned brightly on the hearthstone in the middle of the floor, making shadow shapes on the wooden walls and among the smoky beams of the pointed roof. Hours would pass before Feidhlimí came to join her among the woollen blankets and rugs of fur. Now she would be glad of some time by herself.

"Go to bed, Méabh," she said, smiling at her servant, who could scarcely hide her yawns as she helped the princess to undress and to comb her long, dark hair. "You're going to fall asleep standing up."

The girl went gratefully. Eithne lay down, and the winter night enfolded her.

She had wanted to be alone, but of course she was not alone. Close to her heart there was a baby, whose strong kicks reminded her how soon he would be ready to leave her body and begin to live his own, independent life. At least, Eithne hoped and prayed that it would be "he." She and Feidhlimí would welcome a daughter in the future, but for this child—for whom they had chosen the name Colm, meaning "dove"—they had a special plan. Although he would be born a prince of Ulster, Colm would not grow up to be a king. Instead, his parents intended to give him as a gift to the church, to become a monk, priest, and man of God. They had decided this long ago.

There were many saints in Erin in those days, and it made Eithne proud and excited to think that her son might be one of them, perhaps the greatest of all. As she lay in bed, looking sleepily into the rose-gold heart of the fire, she remembered with a little thrill the old story of St Mochta, who had lived away to the south of Louth, exactly one hundred years before. It was said that when Mochta prayed, he always turned his face to the north, towards Ulster. When his friends asked him why he did this, he replied in a verse that Eithne knew by heart:

A youth shall be born out of the north,
With the rising of the nations;
Erin shall be made fruitful by his flame,
And Albain, friendly to him.

"When will this youth be born?" Mochta's friends wanted to know.

"In a hundred years from now," the saint had replied.

Could St Mochta have been speaking of Colm, Eithne wondered, feeling the child stir within her. Was it possible that he was the youth destined to do great work in his native land, and cross the grey sea to Albain, where some of his own kin, the Scots, had already gone to live? A small voice in Eithne's mind told her that it was so, but she longed for a sign that her son had been specially chosen by God.

Then something wonderful happened.

It seemed to Eithne that she slept for a while. When she woke up, the fire had died down, and the room was dark. There was a stillness, yet also expectancy in the air. Eithne felt her eyes drawn towards the narrow window high up on the wall, a rectangle of deep blue, pierced by a single star. As she watched, the star grew brighter, then larger, pushing back the night blue until pure white light filled the window, beaming a path down to the bed where Eithne lay. Then out of the window, which had become a door to the sky, a tall young man came walking, silver-haired and silver-cloaked, and stood beside her.

Eithne was not afraid. She knew that this was a messenger from God. She sat up, eager to hear what he would tell her.

At first, however, the young man did not speak. From the folds of his cloak he pulled out a robe, the most beautiful Eithne had ever seen, and held it out to her. Gladly she took it, shaking out its rich drapes across the bed, fingering the soft material, which glowed with the colours of a thousand flowers. A sweet, mysterious scent rose from the robe, and Eithne experienced a moment of perfect delight, before the young man reached down and drew it away from her. Tears rose in Eithne's eyes.

"But why?" she burst out angrily. "Why did you let me think it was a gift, if you meant to take it away from me? It isn't fair!"

The young man's smile was kind, but his reply was firm. "Even to be allowed to touch this robe is a gift, Eithne," he told her. "You cannot keep such a wonderful thing. Look!"

He took the hem of the robe between his shining fingers, and suddenly tossed it away from him, up into the air. Eithne saw it drawn back towards the window, as if by an invisible hand, and for a moment the pain of losing it seemed impossible to bear. But then, as the young man vanished, the robe seemed to spread out gloriously across the sky. First it was a meadow studded with flowers, then a great swathe of the earth, with the fertile plains of Erin, and the soaring mountains of Albain, and the sea between.

Eithne gazed, and as the vision faded she heard the young man's voice again, saying, "Eithne, don't be afraid. You and your husband will soon have a fine son. Everyone will know that he is God's chosen friend, and God will give him great work to do." It was the sign she had yearned for. Happiness filled Eithne's heart.

Of course, when she told Feidhlimí next morning what had happened, he laughed. "You were dreaming, my love," he said.

It was what she had expected, and she had to admit that he might be right. But if it was a dream, then a dream was the most vivid experience of Eithne's life.

A few weeks later, on a dark December night, an old man lay dying in the abbey of Monasterboice, which he had founded. His name was Abbot Buite, and these were his last words:

"Tonight a child shall be born, who will be glorious before God and men. Many years from now he will come to this place, and visit my grave. So he and I shall be friends, in Heaven and on earth."

Abbot Buite spoke truly. It was a night of death for him, and birth for another.

These are stories told about the coming of Colm, also called Columba, who was born at Gartan, Co. Donegal, on 7 December in the year 521. As time passed there would be many more, some of them true, some of them legends, about a saint who was also a prince and hero of Ireland. Columba was real, but he was born among people who love to make up stories, and he was the sort of person they loved to make up stories about.

2

Colm of the Church

"Colm Cille! Colm Cille!"

Colm sat in the doorway of his little thatched cell and watched the round, fair heads bobbing up and down behind the hedge. He was half amused, and half annoyed—amused because he knew it was just a game, annoyed because the long summer evening was slipping away into night, and soon it would be too dark to see the psalter that lay open across his knees. If he had to waste precious time chasing intruders ...

"Colm Cille!" They knew that he knew they were there. That was part of the game. "Colm Cille! Churchy Colm!" They knew the risk they were taking, because his temper was famous, and there were nervous giggles behind the hedge. But still Colm didn't move. A moment later three grubby, impudent faces peered right in through a gap in the briars, and Eoghan called mockingly, "And has our little Colm been to church today?"

That did it. Laying the psalter on the ground, Colm leaped over it and shot out through the gate.

Squealing with delight and terror, the three small boys fled before him down the hill, tumbling and jumping barefoot over the warm turf. He caught up with them at the bottom, and they all rolled over together in the long grass, heaving and grunting as they pummelled one another with their brown fists. It didn't take Colm long to get the best of it. It might be three to one, but he was bigger and stronger than they were. Holding Eoghan and Fearghas at arms' length by the hair, and fending off Dáire with his foot, Colm demanded an apology.

"Come on," he panted. "Let's hear it. Loud and clear!"

"Sorry, Colm," chorused the boys, and Colm let them go.

They scurried off to a safe distance, and stood grinning at him. They really liked him, but provoking him was the only way they knew of getting him to play. It was hard to understand someone who seemed only to want to sit indoors reading the Psalms and the Gospels when he might have been out trapping rabbits and playing games in the wood. Colm scowled, but then he grinned back.

"Don't ever make me really angry, though," he warned them. "I might—" But he didn't go on. It frightened him sometimes to think of what he might do.

They stayed on for a while, down by the river, lying on their stomachs on the bank, dropping pebbles to disturb the brown trout lurking in the inky depths of the pools. The moon rose, and owls hooted in the wood. It was almost dark when Dáire's mother came looking for him, and the three boys went off protesting towards the village of wattle huts, a little further upstream. Colm watched them out of sight, then he climbed the hill, and went home.

"Goodnight, my son," called Cruithneachán from his cell, as Colm's moon shadow fell across his door.

"Goodnight, father," replied Colm. He picked up his psalter, bent his back, and passed through the low doorway into his own cell.

Colm could not remember when he had first realised that he was different from other boys. He was eleven now, and he supposed he might have been about four when it dawned on him that all children didn't live with elderly priests, with monthly visits from their mothers. Around the same time he noticed that his mother was not at all like other mothers, the red-faced, shrill-tongued women of the village, with their greasy fair hair, dirty brown tunics, and blackened fingernails. Colm only saw his mother once a month, but she was worth waiting for. He used to stand by the gate of the enclosure as a tiny child, looking eagerly down the road, straining his eyes to see the little dust-cloud far away. Then the white horse, Eathal, would emerge from the dust, with his mother riding pillion behind Aonghas, his father's groom, and fat Méabh on a donkey with the basket of presents, bouncing along behind.

His mother was beautiful, with clean, sweet-smelling braids of dark hair. She wore a long cream robe, and a cloak the colour of blackberry juice, fastened with a gold brooch. She would slide down easily from the horse's high back, and run to him, putting her arms round him and touching his hair.

"Colm! You've grown again! What a good thing I've brought you a new tunic. And look—here are some nut cakes, and a piece of the honeycomb from the Gartan beehives."

Her voice was musical. Colm would take her hand and lead her down to the river, and show her the swan's nest among the reeds. Afterwards she would sit with him, listening proudly as he read to her from the book Cruithneachán had made for him. But always in the late afternoon she rode away again, looking sorrowful in those early days. Now she had other children, and probably missed him less. Colm often heard Cruithneachán call her "Princess," but it was not until he thought to ask the old man what a princess was that he heard, and understood, the whole story. Then he knew how different he was.

Until he was seven, Colm shared Cruithneachán's cell, and it was on a winter evening, while they were sharing their supper of fish and barley bread by the light of the tiny oil-lamp, that the old priest told him what he wanted to know.

Cruithneachán explained what it meant to be a princess, and how Eithne had come from Leinster to marry his father, the chieftain Feidhlimí mac Fearghais, who was a prince, the great-grandson of Niall Naoi-Ghiallach, High King of Erin. He explained too how it was usual for the son of a chieftain like Feidhlimí to be sent as a baby to the house of a less important chief, to be taught to ride, and hunt, and be a warrior.

"But your parents wanted something different for you," said Cruithneachán gently. "Although you are a prince of Erin, and might one day have been chosen to sit upon the throne at Tara of the Kings, they decided before your birth that you were to be, not a warrior but a man of peace. So they sent you here to me, to live in my household and learn the things of God." He paused, then added, "I think they were right."

"Do you? Why?" asked Colm, who was rather regretting the loss of his chance to sit on the throne at Tara of the Kings.

Cruithneachán hesitated for a moment, then he made up his mind. The boy had a right to know. Simply, he told Colm of the vision Eithne had had before he was born, of the robe that had spread across the sky, over all Erin and Albain.

"And another thing," he said. "One night when you were a baby, I left you asleep here in the cell while I went over to the church to pray. When I came out I thought the cell was on fire. Light was shining out of the door, and through the cracks

in the walls. I ran back with my heart in my
mouth, but it wasn't fire, Colm, only light. It was
brightest over the crib where you lay. I was
terrified," admitted the old man.

"Probably the moon," said Colm gruffly.

"God's light is brighter than the moon," replied
Cruithneachán confidently.

Colm said no more, but later, when the lamp
had been extinguished and Cruithneachán was
asleep, he lay curled up under his warm blanket,
and considered what the old man had said. He
decided that he was pleased. It was good to be a
prince, of course, and it might be useful later on.
But he really wanted to be a monk, and to stay
with Cruithneachán, whom he loved far more
than the mother he saw only once a month, and
the father he had never seen. It was fun living with
Cruithneachán, who had taught him to fish, and
to swim, and to play draughts and knucklebones.
Cruithneachán had told him the names of all the
birds, and had once made him a marvellous cake,
with letters on the top, so that he could learn his
alphabet in a delicious way.

As for these stories Cruithneachán had told
him—well, they were hard to believe. Perhaps his
mother had been dreaming, and he knew that in
the vastness of the night the moonshine could be
both bright and eerie. That was what Colm thought,
until a few months later. Then he learnt how other
people's strange experiences are always less
believable than your own.

"Let me hear your lesson," said Cruithneachán to Colm. "Start with *I will lift up mine eyes unto the hills*."

It was a morning in June, and they were going to visit a sick man, who was lying in a hovel on the other side of the wood. High above them the oak leaves drew curly patterns on the blue sky, but down on the forest floor it was dark and wet, and there was a smell of mould. Colm had learnt the psalm the night before. He had a good memory, and didn't forget things.

"I will lift up mine eyes unto the hills," he began obediently, *"from whence cometh my help. My help cometh from the Lord, which made heaven and earth. He will not suffer thy foot to be moved—"*

It did not seem very appropriate that the accident should happen then. Cruithneachán, who was behind Colm, gave a sharp cry of alarm. Before Colm could turn to steady him Cruithneachán had lost his footing on the slippery path. He fell heavily, cracking his head on a boulder, and lay perfectly still.

Colm knew the sensible thing to do. He should run for help, either back to the village by the river or forward to the nunnery, where half a dozen good sisters lived in cells planted around the little wooden church. But he didn't. Instead, acting as if someone else were manipulating him, he did something extraordinary. Taking off his cloak, he rolled it up and slid it gently under Cruithneachán's grey head as a pillow. Then he sat down among the acorns beside him, and went on reciting his lesson in a loud, clear voice.

"He that keepeth thee will not slumber ... The Lord is thy keeper: the Lord is thy shade upon thy right hand." He was saying it to Cruithneachán. "Don't be afraid, father."

The nuns heard him. They came running along the path on sandalled feet, holding up their heavy skirts out of the mud. Like anxious brown hens, they circled the unconscious old man and the chanting child.

"It's Father Cruithneachán."

"And Colm."

"What are you doing, Colm?"

"Sh!" Sister Maghna bent over the crumpled body and put her right hand inside Cruithneachán's habit, over his heart. When she straightened up, her lips were trembling. "I think he's dead," she whispered.

Colm looked up, around the circle of white, frightened faces. He heard himself say calmly, "No. He is not dead. Leave this to me."

That was when he felt the strong, strange power flow into him. He was only a little boy, but that power would be his until his dying day. Kneeling by Cruithneachán, he touched the thin grey hair, and took the cold, dry hand in his.

"Wake up, father," said Colm lovingly. "I haven't finished my lesson yet."

Cruithneachán opened his eyes, and they smiled at each other.

3

Columba

The May morning dawned with a fine concert by the birds. As he dressed for the very last time in his little wooden cell, Colm automatically picked out the familiar notes. There was the song-thrush, Cruithneachán's favourite. That was the robin, and there were the hedge-sparrow and the chaffinch. The willow-warbler was sitting on the thatch; overhead Colm could hear his sweet "Soo-oo-ee! Soo-oo-ee!" And as he stepped out, curling his toes as the cold, dewy grass invaded his sandals, he saw his own favourite blackbird on the hedge, singing his farewell through the morning mist. Colm thought his heart would break.

Of course he had always known that he could not stay for ever at Kilmacrenan with Cruithneachán. Although they were bound to each other as father and son for as long as they both lived, Colm would have to leave, to continue his education elsewhere. He was sixteen now, and had mastered all that Cruithneachán could teach him. The time had come for him to say goodbye to the old priest and set out on the long journey that would be his life. One part of him was ready, and excited. But the house of Cruithneachán was the only home he had ever known. For the last two weeks he had been wandering sadly through the spring-green woods, and along the river banks, trying desperately to imprint on his memory beautiful scenes that he did not expect to see again.

"You'll feel better when you're on your way," said Cruithneachán, coming out of his cell. He was old, and had learnt to hide his sorrow. He was carrying the brown leather bag he had packed for Colm's journey with bread and cheese and the last russet apples from the winter store.

Colm nodded. He dared not look at the kind old face. "Thanks," he said gruffly, as he slipped his precious psalter into the bag and tied the thongs around its neck.

"I'll come with you as far as the ford," Cruithneachán said.

The sun was rising as they walked together down the hill, the stooping old man in his rough woollen habit and the upright youth in his tunic of much finer wool. The eastern sky flushed, and ribbons of mist began to disperse over the river. It was going to be a beautiful day. Colm and Cruithneachán did not speak. They had sat up talking late into the night, and there was no more to say. On silent feet they padded along the green river bank, past the sleeping village, and came all too soon to the ford. Colm couldn't have spoken if he had tried.

"God go with you, my dear son," said Cruithneachán. "Don't be anxious about me. Your parents will look after me, just as I've looked after you. Go in peace, and remember my words—Columba."

In spite of his grief, Colm smiled. He took the old man in his arms, and held him in a strong, quick embrace. They would send each other messages from time to time, but he knew they would never meet again. Then he crossed the Leannan and, without looking back, plunged into the woods on the other side.

Cruithneachán had been right. Once the terrible moment of parting was over, and he was into his stride, Colm's spirits lifted. As he stepped eastward by river and lough, finding the narrow paths through moorland and wood, he began to enjoy himself. It was a great adventure, after all, to be on his way to Fionnbharr's monastery school at Moville, where he would learn new lessons, and make new friends of his own age, who shared his interests—unlike those scamps Eoghan, Fearghas, and Dáire, he thought, who had called him "Churchy Colm" to the last. But every so often these happy reflections were disturbed by the memory of his dear foster-father Cruithneachán, and for a while the sun seemed less bright and the grass less green, and the birdsong faded in his ears.

The previous night Colm and Cruithneachán had sat up very late. When there was no oil left in the lamp and the tiny flame died, they had gone on talking in the dark.

"Tell me, Colm. If God offered you three gifts, what would you ask him for?"

Colm thought for a moment. Then, "I would ask for chastity, wisdom, and pilgrimage," he replied.

"I see," said the old man. "Chastity. Do you know what that means, Colm?"

Colm knew that it meant he could never have a wife to love, or children. He must give up for ever the longing he sometimes felt for the warmth and comfort of family life, which he knew existed but had never shared. Neither he nor any son of his would sit on the throne at Tara of the Kings. He must take God as his only friend, and keep himself free for God's service.

"Yes, I do," he said.

"It is hard to live alone with God," said Cruithneachán. "But God will grant you this gift. Let's take pilgrimage next. You'd like to travel?"

"Oh, yes," said Colm, who had never been further than nearby Temple Douglas in his life.

"Where?" asked Cruithneachán.

Ever since they had entertained an old friend of Cruithneachán's who had just returned from a pilgrimage to Rome, Colm had thought how exciting such a journey would be. He imagined himself going aboard a curach, and crossing the sea from Erin to Brittany. Then he would travel south through Burgundy, cross the ice-pinnacled Alps, and see below him the sun-soaked Lombardy plain. Pressing on under an ever intenser blue sky, he would come at last to the holy city of Rome. Or instead he might sail east, to the misty land of Albain, which his mother had seen in a vision before he was born. But, "I would go where God sent me, father," he said firmly.

Cruithneachán was pleased with this answer. "God will give you this gift too," he said. He paused, then went on, "But wisdom? Oh, Colm! For you, wisdom will be very hard to attain."

Colm felt slightly peeved. "I don't know," he sniffed. "I think I'm fairly wise."

He heard Cruithneachán laughing softly in the darkness. "I'm sorry to contradict you," was the reply. "You're a good, kind, affectionate lad, but you're a haughty prince at heart. The first wise thing you could do would be to learn to keep your temper."

Colm sighed. It was true, of course. He was proud of being a prince, and his temper was awful. "I'll try," he promised.

"I hope you will," said the old priest seriously. "God has given you great power, as I know better than anyone, since I owe my life to it. But he has left you free to choose how to use it, which is why you need wisdom more than anything else. If you were to get into a rage, and use your power rashly, you could be dangerous. Do you understand, Colm?"

Colm shivered. He had been afraid of his power ever since he first realised he had it. Cruithneachán was saying nothing he hadn't thought himself a thousand times. "Yes," he whispered.

Cruithneachán sighed. "I cannot tell whether God will grant your wish for wisdom," he said. "You must pray for it from day to day." Then the tone of his voice changed, and Colm knew he was smiling in the dark. "Perhaps you ought to change your name," he added.

"Change my name?" repeated Colm, puzzled.

"In Latin," Cruithneachán reminded him, "your name would be Columba, which also means 'dove'—the bird of peace. If you were called that, you might remember to live up to your name."

Colm had thought it funny at the time. But next day, as he sat at noon at the edge of a stream, paddling his feet and lunching on Cruithneachán's bread and cheese, it seemed like a good idea after all. A new name for a new life, and he liked the sound of it. He could not know then that Columba would be his "Sunday name." One day, through all the lands of Erin and Albain, he would also be known by the name his playmates at Kilmacrenan had given him and that had annoyed him when he was a little boy: "Colm Cille"—Colm of the Church.

4

Death in the Plain

The two years Columba spent at Moville as a pupil of Abbot Fionnbharr were happy ones. The rough wooden cell he built for himself in the grassy enclosure beside the church was just like the one he had always lived in, and in some ways his life had scarcely changed. But there were new lessons to learn, and an opportunity to take pen, ink and parchment and begin to make beautiful copies of the Psalms and the Gospels. Columba loved this work more than anything else. He loved the scratching of the pen, the fun of making twirly patterns around the initial letters, the satisfaction of watching lines of neatly rounded letters flowing out from under his right hand. He couldn't keep away from it. Every spare minute was spent copying, and when Abbot Fionnbharr praised his work, he was overjoyed.

Often Columba remembered Cruithneachán's parting advice, and he did try to control his temper. Sometimes he succeeded, sometimes not. When Fionnbharr discovered that Columba had healing in his hands, he brought sick people to him, and Columba gladly helped them. He kept to himself his fear that his power might have a darker, more destructive side.

After two years with Fionnbharr, Columba had learnt enough to become a deacon, which was the first step to becoming a priest. The top of his head was shaved, in the shape of a leaf, from ear to ear, and he exchanged his fine tunic and princely cloak for a long habit of rough wool. More study was required before he could become a priest, and it was arranged that he would go on to the monastery school of the great Abbot Finnian at Clonard in Leinster. On the way he would spend time with his parents' friend, the bard Geamán, who would teach him the ancient legends of his people, and how to speak in public.

This seemed to Columba a good idea. Since St Patrick's time, many people in Erin had gone back to the dark, heathen ways their ancestors had followed before he came. If Columba were to preach the Gospel to them, as he intended to do, it would be sensible to learn how to speak in a way that would make them want to listen. So, two years after he had said goodbye to Cruithneachán, Columba said goodbye now to Fionnbharr. In his monk's habit and with a rough grey blanket to serve him as a cloak, he travelled south from Ulster, through the green heartland of Erin into Leinster, where his mother, Eithne, had lived long ago.

"Let us take a walk this morning," said Geamán after breakfast. "We can take our work with us, and spend a pleasant hour in the sunshine."

It was September, and Columba could scarcely believe that he had been with the old bard for almost six months. He had had a wonderful time, reading and listening to marvellous stories about Cú Chulainn and Oisín, Fionn and Oscar, and Niall Naoi-Ghiallach, his own great-great-grandfather. It had been fun, and the old tales had been a refreshing change from anything he had ever learnt before. He felt prouder than ever to realise that he was of the race of Conall Gulban, and descended from people worth making up poetry about. Columba was quite sad when he remembered that in a month's time he must leave this new friend and move on again, to Clonard.

"I'll put my sandals on," he said eagerly, scooping up the last of the porridge in his wooden bowl with his fingers and cramming it into his mouth. "Where shall we go?"

"Into the plain," said Geamán. "As far as my old legs will carry me."

It was like walking with Cruithneachán, Columba thought, as he slowed his steps to keep pace with the old man's shuffle. Geamán said he didn't know how old he was, but Eithne, who had known him all her life, reckoned he was over eighty. Outside the wattle fence that protected the bard's thatched house, the plain of Meath rolled away, its summer green now flushed with autumn colours. The king's hill and hall at Tara were visible across the Boyne.

Geamán could not walk far, and soon he was looking for a place to sit down. There was a sheltered spot out of the wind, between a hillock and a little wood; Geamán sat down on a flat-topped boulder, while Columba threw himself down on the grass, lying on his back to watch the clouds tumbling across the windy sky.

"You might let me hear the tale of the Fate of the Children of Lir," suggested Geamán. "I know it, to be sure, but I may as well find out if you do."

Columba grinned, and sat up. But before he could open his mouth to speak, something terrible occurred.

First, there was a commotion in the wood nearby. A high voice was screaming, "No! Please, don't kill me! Leave me alone!" A deep, harsh voice shouted in reply, "Come back here! Try to escape from me, would you! I'll show you how I deal with runaway slaves!"

There was a crashing and blundering in the undergrowth, then suddenly a girl of about fourteen, dressed in rags and with tangled hair falling around her tear-stained face, broke from the wood like a hunted deer. Seeing Geamán and Columba, she rushed towards them. But even as Geamán threw his cloak over her to hide her, a huge, thick-limbed fellow with bristling black hair lumbered out from the trees. He was carrying a spear, and he was in a terrible rage.

"Leave her alone. She's mine!" he bawled, thundering towards Columba and Geamán, waving his spear.

"Help me, Columba," cried Geamán, but Columba was unarmed. Bravely he did what he could. Stepping in front of the old man, he threw his cloak too over the whimpering girl. It was no use. Pushing Columba aside, so that he staggered and fell, the evil man pulled the cloaks away, and speared the girl through the heart.

Columba got up. Fury was gripping him like a sharp-nailed hand at his throat. He felt the power that had revived Cruithneachán rise up in him again, but this time he wanted to use it in a completely different way. Facing the murderer, he cried in a loud voice, "You villain! At the same hour at which this innocent girl's soul goes up into Heaven, yours will go down to Hell!"

He saw the man's eyes widen, first in stupid incredulity, then in fear. His bearded mouth gaped, and his face went purple. He choked. Then he fell dead at Geamán's feet.

Columba had always known that he could kill someone. Now he had.

5

The Golden Moon

Geamán said it was all right. He pointed out that the dead man had been a cruel keeper of slaves, and a cold-blooded murderer. Columba had used his power properly in killing him. No-one knowing the facts could think otherwise. Because he wanted to, Columba believed him, but far down, in an uneasy corner of his mind, he knew that he had used his power in a moment of blind fury. However much the murderer had deserved his fate, Columba had struck him down without really thinking what he was doing. With all his heart, he wished that God had given him only the power to do good. But he knew that that was not God's way.

For the moment, however, the deed made him famous. Geamán was a chatterbox. It was not long before the news of what had happened spread, first among the bard's friends, then through all the land. When Columba arrived at nearby Clonard to continue his studies, he found that his fellow-students—and there were three thousand of them—all knew who he was. They treated him with a

respect that he was vain enough to feel was due
to a prince of the house of Conall Gulban. But he
knew it also had something to do with a fear that
if they displeased him they might also fall down
dead. Columba was amused and ashamed at the
same time.

While he was at Clonard, however, the belief
grew in him that he had been chosen to do some
great work for God.

Columba had never in all his life seen a place
like the monastery that Finnian ruled over at
Clonard. Villages and monasteries in Erin were
tiny in those days, with great swathes of beautiful
but empty land between them. The monastery at
Clonard was more like a city. Finnian had once
longed to go on pilgrimage to Rome, but it was
said that an angel had appeared to him, saying,
"God doesn't need you in Rome. Arise, and renew
the faith of Erin, after Patrick." So Finnian founded
a monastery and school at Clonard. He was a
brilliant teacher. Students flocked to the school,
and he never turned anyone away. But apart from
its vast size, Clonard was just like any other monastery, with a church built of oak wood, barns, dining-
hall, and bakery, and cells like wooden beehives
crowding the spaces in between. A ráth, or rampart,
topped by a wooden fence, surrounded the
enclosure, and outside there were fields, where the
students planted crops and kept sheep and cattle.

"Where shall I build my cell, father?" Columba
asked Finnian when the abbot had welcomed him

and asked for news of his family and Geamán. Columba liked this tall, energetic monk with his golden beard and bright, shrewd blue eyes.

"There's a space outside the church door that will do," replied Finnian. He laughed, and added, "Very handy with winter coming on. You won't get soaked to the skin on your way to service. I'll get Ciarán to help you."

Ciarán was stout and cheerful, with a round pink face and a mat of soft brown hair between his forehead and his leaf-shaped tonsure. He looked with interest at the tall, red-haired stranger. The two young men liked each other at once, and would be friends for the rest of their lives.

"You can leave your bag and cloak in my cell while we build yours," said Ciarán. "We've a store of wood and wattles outside the gate, and later we'll fetch mud from the river bank to seal the walls."

Columba happily shouldered a bundle of wood, and Ciarán another. They walked back across the ráth, Ciarán stopping occasionally to introduce Columba to other students who happened to be passing. "This is Breandán. This is Comhghall. This is Cainneach. I'd like you to meet Columba."

The young monks were pleasant, and Columba thought he would like it here. But when they arrived at the place where Abbot Finnian had said the cell was to be built, Columba felt there was something wrong. Surely the abbot had made a mistake? "Sorry. Not here," he said firmly to Ciarán, who was laying down his burden of wood. "My cell should be over there, in front of the guesthouse. Come on, Ciarán."

Ciarán listened to the imperious voice in astonishment. This man was a deacon. Surely he knew by now that monks had to obey their abbot's instructions? Ciarán knew Columba was a prince, but he couldn't help feeling that perhaps the new student was too big for his sandals. Still, it wasn't his affair. Shrugging his shoulders, he followed Columba, and in front of the guesthouse, fifty paces from the church door, the cell was built.

They had woven the walls and daubed them with mud and were trimming the thatch when Finnian passed by on his way to the church. Ciarán managed to melt away among the cells, and Columba was left to face his abbot's displeasure alone.

"This is a bad start," said Finnian sternly. "Why have you disobeyed me, Columba?"

Columba was not afraid. "Father," he said, "soon this great monastery of yours will be even greater. Soon the church will be far too small to hold all the people who will come to hear the preaching of God's word. It will have to be made twice as large. I have built my cell where the door of the new, larger church will be." And before Finnian could speak, he added hastily, "Please believe me, father. Sometimes—I know things."

Finnian looked into the fearless grey eyes. He had heard how Columba had avenged the runaway

slave in the plain of Meath. He knew that this was
no ordinary student. "All right," he said. "We'll let
it pass this time. But try to be obedient in future."

"Yes, father," Columba replied.

That night Abbot Finnian had a dream. In a
dark blue sky he saw two moons. A golden one,
to the north, shone brightly over both Erin and
Albain, while a silver one shed a paler, gentler light
over the Shannon to the south. When he awoke,
Finnian knew at once what the dream meant. The
golden moon represented Columba. The silver
moon represented his new friend, Ciarán, who also
had work to do for God in Erin. But Columba's
moon shed the intenser light.

Columba stayed four years at Finnian's school,
studying hard and making yet more beautiful copies
of the Psalms and the Gospels. He attended classes.
He worked in the fields, and helped to rebuild the
church. As he had prophesied, it had to be enlarged,
and by the final summer of his stay his cell was
indeed outside its door. He tried to keep his temper,
and be humble, but these things were as hard for
him as they had ever been.

When Finnian told him of his dream, Columba
was secretly thrilled that his was the golden moon
while Ciarán's was only silver. (Ciarán was delighted
to have a moon at all.) Columba was proud to be
known as the cleverest student in the school, and
thought it was no more than he deserved. And
when the other students did odd jobs for him,

because he was a prince, he did not stop them, as he knew he ought to have done. Even a crazy story that spread through the monastery, that an angel came every night to grind his corn, because he was too grand to do it himself, privately pleased him. Cruithneachán would have said he still had a lot to learn.

At the end of his fourth year, however, Columba was ordained priest by Bishop Eachtan of Clonfert. The same evening, Finnian sent for him to have a last talk.

"Of all my students," he said, "I have chosen the best twelve, of whom you are one. These are bad times in Erin. Too many people have forgotten the true faith that Patrick taught, and have gone back to worshipping false gods and listening to their evil servants, the druids. Your job will be to found monasteries, preach the Gospel, and make Erin a Christian land once more."

Finnian did not tell Columba of his belief that one day he would be the greatest of the twelve. He thought that, for all his good qualities, Columba was conceited enough already.

The next morning, Columba left Clonard with Ciarán and two other friends, Cainneach and Comhghall.

"I'm sending you to Glasnevin," Finnian had said, "to stay with Mobhí Cláiríneach for a while. Before you start setting up monasteries of your own, it will do you good to see how one of the finest men in Erin runs his."

6

Mobhí

At first sight, Mobhí Cláiríneach was a horror.
There was no other word for it. When the four
young men met him at the gate of his little
monastery on the bank of the Tolka River, they
were glad he couldn't see their expressions. Their
feeling of shock and revulsion was impossible to
hide. A terrible accident when he was a baby had
left Mobhí not only blind but eyeless, and with a
red-rimmed hole in his face where his nose should
have been. His mouth was normal, but when he
spoke his low, melodious voice seemed out of
keeping with his ruin of a face.

"You are welcome to Glasnevin, young brothers,"
he said. "We've all been looking forward to your
coming, haven't we, Bearchán?"

The words were addressed to a thin boy of
about twelve, who was holding Mobhí's hand and
looking up affectionately into the terrible face.

"Yes, father," he said, and smiled at the new-
comers. "You'll be very happy here," he added
reassuringly.

Bearchán was right. Mobhí was a kind and just abbot, and his monastery was a place of friendship and peace. It had never been clearer to Columba that if you wanted to influence people, encouragement was more effective than punishment, humility more impressive than pride. Soon, like the other monks and students, who lived in fifty cells on the opposite side of the river from the church, Columba stopped noticing Mobhí's hideous appearance. It was the thing that mattered least about him.

Columba would have done anything to please Mobhí. One night in spring, when the Tolka was in spate after heavy rain, the bell rang for Matins in the church on the opposite side. Grumbling and shivering in the darkness, the students crept out of their cells and gathered on the brink of the growling, swirling water. The wind roared, tossing pellets of icy rain into their faces, and they were afraid.

"I'm not going to cross a flood like that at midnight," said Comhghall indignantly.

"Nor me," agreed Cainneach. "I don't want to be drowned. They'll just have to say Matins without me, for once."

There was a loud murmur of agreement. Surely no-one could be expected to cross such a dangerous torrent in the dark. The students went back to bed—all except Columba.

Columba knew that monks ought to trust God, and he was determined not to let Mobhí down. Hitching up his habit, he stepped down into the water, and began to make his way across. The black, icy waves sucked hungrily around him, trying to unbalance him. Several times he lost his footing on the slippery stones, and almost fell into the flood. He lost a sandal. But he pressed on, and at last, soaked to the skin, he stumbled onto the bank on the other side.

"Here comes Brother Columba, father!" cried Bearchán's young voice as Columba staggered over the grass towards the church.

Mobhí was standing in the doorway, outlined by the faint glow of the lamp within. "Well done, Columba," he said. "I knew you would come."

In spite of his cold, dripping garments and the pain of a badly cut foot, Columba felt warm again.

Sadly, Columba's time with Mobhí was very short. He had intended to stay for a year, in the hope that some of Mobhí's gentleness and goodness might rub off permanently on him. But one day, after Columba had been only a few months at Glasnevin, Mobhí called his monks and students to a meeting in the church. There he broke to them some terrible news.

"Brothers and sons," he said, "I know that you will be troubled by what I have to tell you, but we must all trust in God. Yesterday, I was called to visit a sick boy in the village over the hill. While I was with him, he died—of the yellow plague." He paused, as a great gasp of horror rose from the young men. They looked at each other with wide, frightened eyes, and only the bravest managed to appear calm. "I have heard of other deaths," went on Mobhí, "and I have decided to close our monastery and school. You will be safer if you separate and get well away from this district for a while."

Columba was grief-stricken as he packed his few belongings and left his cell. He knew that Mobhí was being wise, although this parting was hard to bear. Everyone was afraid of the plague, and rightly so. It was an appalling illness. First the skin of the sufferer turned yellow, and a terrible cough and fever racked his body. Then painful swellings rose in his groin and armpits, and when these burst a deathly stench filled the air. By the time the wretched victim died he had probably infected his whole family and any kind monk who had come to pray beside him. Columba feared for his beloved Mobhí, and he had wild thoughts of offering to stay, in case his healing gifts could be of use to him. But he knew that Mobhí would never agree. He would trust God, whether he lived or died.

"Columba," said Mobhí when Columba came to say goodbye to him, "I have a last instruction for you, which I know you will obey. You must go north now to your own land of Ulster—but please, do not accept land for your first monastery from anyone until you have my permission. When the time comes, I shall know what is God's will for you. Will you promise?"

"Gladly," replied Columba.

He did not ask what he should do if Mobhí died of plague before giving his permission—that was not the kind of question one could ask. But perhaps Mobhí knew what he was thinking, because he added firmly, "I'll send word to you, whatever happens. Trust me."

Trusting Mobhí was the easiest thing Columba had ever had to do.

They walked together to the gate, Mobhí finding his way with his hand on Columba's shoulder. There they hugged each other, and Columba gently touched Mobhí's disfigured face.

"Goodbye," he said. "I've learnt a lot here. Thank you for everything."

"Go in peace," Mobhí replied.

Columba crossed the river and walked quickly along the footpath, past the forlorn, deserted cells. Where the path entered the wood, he turned and looked back. Mobhí was still at the gate, with his faithful attendant Bearchán again at his side. Columba waved, and Mobhí, guided by Bearchán, waved back. Then Columba turned north, and set out on another journey.

7

The Little Oak-Grove

It was spring once more. After the long night of
winter, the woods were cheerful with birdsong.
Streams gabbled, released from the silencing grip
of ice, and small beasts scurried in the undergrowth.
Usually Columba loved this season of promise,
relishing its fresh green smells, enjoying the tender
beauty of the opening leaves. But this year he
could find no pleasure in these things. Sickness lay
over the land, in horrible contrast to nature's
health. Often as Columba passed near a village, a
poor soul came running to ask him to come and
comfort the dying, and more than once he was
turned away from a monastery where he hoped to
spend the night.

"Sleep in a ditch, brother," a frightened voice
would call from behind the gate. "You will be safer
there than you would be here tonight."

Columba was not afraid for himself. He believed
that he had work to do for God and that God
would preserve his life until that work was done.
But he grieved for the suffering of others, and he

was afraid that he might be a plague-carrier, who would spread the disease among his own people.

One day Columba came to a river, then called the Búir, which crossed his path from west to east. Tired and anxious, he knelt on the bank, closed his eyes, and prayed. "Please, God," he said, "don't let the plague cross this river. Save my people, who live to the north of it."

God heard Columba's prayer, and answered it. The lands of Erin north of the Búir escaped the plague at that time.

When Columba came at last to his homeland, he went straight to the fort of Aodh, son of Ainmhire, King of Ulster and a chief of Columba's own clan, the Uí Néill. In fact Aodh was his cousin, and he received a very kindly welcome. It was wonderful, after so long on the road, to bathe and put on clean clothes, to eat a proper meal, and to look forward to a long sleep in a comfortable bed. A monk's life was very hard, and such luxuries rarely came Columba's way. In the evening a feast was held in his honour, with fine food, wine, and music. Afterwards the two cousins retired to Aodh's private room to talk.

"I have a favour to ask," Columba said, as Aodh refilled their goblets with wine and sat down in his carved oak chair by the fire.

"If I can," agreed Aodh, looking thoughtfully at his tall, keen-faced cousin. In spite of his plain monk's habit, Columba looked every inch a prince.

Aodh had never met him before, but he had heard of him, and was anxious not to offend a man who, it was said, could raise the dead and strike down the living.

"I need a place to build a monastery," Columba told him. "If I am to spread the word of God in Erin I must have a base, a place where I can train my helpers, and—" He prevented himself from adding, "Somewhere I can call home," but it was what he meant. He had never had a home since he left Cruithneachán's house seven years before, and after so much moving around, he longed for a place of his own.

Aodh nodded. He was relieved that the request was so easy to grant.

"Of course," he said. "I know the very place for you—a fort of mine at Derry. Why don't you go and look at it tomorrow? If you think it will suit you, we can make an arrangement straight away."

Columba was delighted, and thanked Aodh warmly. Only later, when he was in bed, did he realise that there was a snag. He had promised Mobhí that he would not accept land from anyone without his permission. Oh, dear, he thought. This could be awkward. It would be very difficult explaining to Aodh that he had to wait for a message from another monk, miles away in the south, before he could decide whether or not to accept this generous gift. Columba knew from his own experience that princes could be quick-tempered. Suppose Aodh was haughty and went into a huff, and withdrew the offer? Eventually, Columba decided that he would go and look at the site at nearby Derry in the morning. After that he would decide what to do. Then he fell asleep.

As soon as Columba saw the hill at Derry, rising out of a little oak-wood, with a clear stream running by, he wanted it more than he had ever wanted anything in his life. It was so peaceful, the quiet broken only by the gentle sounds he loved: the chuckling of water, the breeze whispering in the branches, the shy, throaty call of wood-pigeons among the leaves.

Columba climbed up over the mossy grass towards Aodh's little wooden fort. It would have to go, of course, and be replaced with a church. Sitting on a stone, Columba happily planned his monastery. He would build his own cell apart, under the eaves of the wood, with his guesthouse opposite, across the stream. When other monks came to join him, they could build their cells on a greensward at the bottom of the hill. By the water there would be a mill, and beyond it a kiln for drying the barley.

Soon Columba had his monastery built in the eye of his imagination. He was putting the finishing touches to his plan when he again remembered his promise to Mobhí. It had been easy to trust Mobhí at the time, but now he couldn't help wishing he had never made the promise at all. What was he to do? A cloud seemed to blow across the sun.

Sadly, Columba came down from the hill and passed through the oak-wood. He knew he must keep his promise; monks had to be obedient, and no man could look for blessing who broke his word to a friend. He must go back to Aodh and say, "I'm sorry, I can't accept your offer," even though he knew that Aodh would probably never make him another.

Columba was so unhappy, walking with bent head, that he did not see the two figures approaching until they were almost upon him. The sharp snap of a twig under someone's foot alerted him, and he looked up, startled. At once his surprise deepened into astonishment. A young monk and a thin, tear-stained boy stood in front of him on the path. He knew them well. The monk, one of Mobhí's followers at Glasnevin, was called Lua. The boy was Mobhí's helper, Bearchán.

It was Bearchán who spoke. "Oh, Brother Columba," he cried, with tears running down his cheeks, "Father Mobhí is dead! He died of plague, soon after you left us. Now I have no friend. What shall I do?"

Columba laid his hand on Bearchán's fair head. He looked at Lua, who was also close to tears. "Is there a message for me?" he asked, struggling to keep his voice steady.

Lua nodded. "Father Mobhí sent you his blessing. You are to accept the land that King Aodh has offered you for your monastery. And here is Father Mobhí's girdle, as a token of his love."

Columba took the rough, horsehair girdle reverently, as though it were the gift of a king.

"It's all right, Bearchán," he said kindly. "Don't cry any more. I'll be your friend. You can stay with me."

Long years afterwards, another monk would write of Columba that he could never spend a single hour without study, or prayer, or writing, or some other holy occupation. His energy was amazing, and now it was all directed towards building his monastery at Derry. Perhaps God rewarded him for his obedience to Mobhí, because for a while everything went well for him. Lua and Bearchán were his first helpers, but soon others came, and through the summer they worked together, building the church and cells, ploughing the fields outside the ráth, making pens for the sheep and cattle King Aodh had given them. Columba was happy, and if occasionally he still lost his temper, more often he managed to control it. The lessons he had learnt by watching Mobhí Cláiríneach helped him to be kind and just in his own dealings with others.

One sunny morning when the church was half built, the monks came to Columba and told him that they had run out of wattles, the willow twigs they were using to weave the walls.

"Go into the wood on the other side of the hill," ordered Columba. "Cut as many as you need."

The monks went off, returning after a while with great bundles of twigs, but also with a story. "While we were cutting the wattles," Lua told Columba, who was sitting at the door of his cell copying a manuscript, "a young fellow pounced out on us in a great rage. He said the wood belonged to him, and we had no right to cut timber without his permission."

Columba put down his pen. "What did you do?" he asked.

Lua grinned. "We told him we didn't need his permission, since we had yours," he replied.

Not long before, Columba would have agreed heartily. He would have thought that because he was a prince he could cut wattles anywhere he liked. But living with Mobhí had made him humbler, and now he saw that the young man had reason to be annoyed.

"We still have some of the barley grain that King Aodh gave us," he said. "Take the young man the value of his wattles in barley seed, and tell him to plant it."

"Now?" asked Lua doubtfully. It was high summer, and long past the time for planting seed.

"Now," said Columba firmly, lifting his pen again.

Lua shrugged his shoulders, but not until he was safely behind the fence. He took the grain to the young man with Columba's instructions, and if the young man, who was a farmer, thought the instructions were crazy, he still carried them out.

He too had heard of Columba, the man with power.

Four weeks later, at Lammastide, the young farmer came to the monastery to thank Columba. "My fields are full of beautiful yellow barley," he said. "And can you believe it, Abbot Columba? The grain you gave me in exchange for my wattles has grown taller, riper and finer than the crop I planted in the spring! It's like a miracle."

"It is a miracle," Columba replied.

By the autumn, when the curly oak leaves turned crisp and gold, and red berries nodded in the hedgerow, Columba's monastery was complete. The walls of the church and cells had been daubed with mud, and the thatch weighted with stones to keep it firm against the winter storms. Columba was delighted with it. Even when winter unleaved the wood and the icicles hung like long teeth from the thatch, he was happy. He enjoyed the mist creeping up the lough from the sea, and the rose-red sun, hanging like a lantern above the horizon. He forgot the misery of colds and chilblains when he listened to the hooting owls, or saw a spider's web, stiffened by the frost into a shape of mysterious beauty. Columba had never known comfort, so he didn't miss it, and he had an eye for beautiful things. Often he regretted asking God to grant him pilgrimage. These days, travel was the last thing he wanted. He could have stayed contentedly at Derry for the rest of his days.

It was a vain desire, of course. During the next ten years, as one of Finnian's chosen twelve, Columba travelled far through Erin. Part of the gift God had given him was the power to persuade, and when he preached the Gospel, many people turned from their heathen beliefs to faith in Christ. He begged land from other kings and princes, and founded new monasteries at Kells, Durrow, Moone, Swords, and Kilmore. Away into the north-west he journeyed, to found a monastery on the lonely Donegal coast, which in those days was thought to be the edge of the world. The place where it stood still bears his name. It is called Gleann Cholm Cille. But wherever he went, he longed to return to his first monastery at Derry, which he would always love more than any other place on earth.

Once, when he was far away and homesick, Columba wrote a poem about it:

...The reason I love Derry is
For its quietness, for its purity,
And for its crowds of white angels
From one end to the other.
The reason I love Derry is
For its quietness, for its purity.
Crowded full of Heaven's angels
Is every leaf of the oaks of Derry.
My Derry, my little oak-grove,
My dwelling, and my little cell...

Because he was busy, and happy, Columba found it easy to behave well. He felt that God was close to him, and the kind, loving side of his nature was uppermost in those years. He used his power wisely, to heal the sick and to help those who were in trouble. He did not forget that he had once killed a man, but, now that he did not fly into a rage so frequently, he forgot to guard against the dark side of his power. Which was a pity, as things turned out. Unfortunately the day was approaching when he would lose his temper very spectacularly indeed.

8

A Quarrel at Moville

Columba loved books. He loved the feel of the parchment, the smell of the ink, the mystery of symbols forming words as they marched along the line. Long before printing was invented he was busy in every spare moment, copying the Psalms and the Gospels, making books to give as presents to churches and to the monasteries he had founded. It was said that he founded three hundred monasteries, and wrote three hundred books!

Such a gift was a great honour, and soon stories were being told about the miraculous quality of books "written by the dear and holy fingers of Columba." Such books, it was said, could come undamaged through fire and flood while the leather bags that held them were utterly destroyed. So it was sad that a book got Columba into the worst trouble of his whole life.

It was a day in August, and Columba was on his way back to Derry from a tour of monasteries in the south. Late in the afternoon he found himself close to Fionnbharr's monastery at Moville, on the shores of Lough Foyle.

"Let's go and visit Fionnbharr," he said on impulse to Bearchán and Lua, who were with him. "We'll hear his news, stay overnight in his guest–house, and travel on tomorrow."

Bearchán and Lua were delighted. The day had been stiflingly hot. Now dark thunderclouds were unrolling themselves across the sky, eating up the blue. It would be good to be indoors before the rain started bouncing off the lough, and soaking them to the skin.

Fionnbharr was overjoyed to see his old friend and pupil. Columba and his followers were given water to wash their hot feet, and a meal of bread and fresh fish. The storm broke while the monks were at evening service in the church; rain thrummed like a thousand tapping fingers on the roof, and thunderclaps drowned the singing of the monks as flashes of sheet lightning whitened their startled faces. Bearchán was afraid, but Columba enjoyed the storm. He heard God's voice in the thunder, and when all nature was in uproar the peace inside him felt even more secure. "*O ye lightnings and clouds, bless ye the Lord. Praise him, and magnify him for ever.*"

He had had a good journey. The monasteries were flourishing, his monks were in good heart. He had done something he had intended to do for years and visited the grave of old Abbot Buite of Monasterboice, who had, his mother firmly believed, prophesied greatness for him on the night of his birth. Columba smiled into his clasped hands at the thought of Eithne, grey-haired now but as beautiful as ever, so proud of him, so determined that every prophecy should be fulfilled. *"Oh, let the earth bless the Lord. Yea, let it praise him, and magnify his name for ever."*

Columba was happy and serene. Tomorrow he would go on his way to Derry, to his little oakgrove.

Before the service ended, the storm blew itself away over the sea. The evening sun shone, and the monks stepped from the church onto cool, rain-scented grass. Columba was about to follow Lua and Bearchán back to the guesthouse, but Fionn-bharr touched his arm.

"Wait," he said. "I have something to show you."

When all the other monks were gone he went over to a stone ambry, or cupboard, built against the church's oaken wall. Columba watched as Fionnbharr carefully lifted out a book and laid it open on a reading-desk nearby. Then he fetched a lamp, and held it up so that the pale light spilled over the intricately patterned page.

Columba stared at the book. Then he ran trembling fingers over the creamy pages, marvelling at the finely coloured initials and the lovely flowing script. Never had his beloved Psalms looked so beautiful. Columba felt the soft leather binding, and sniffed its special, bookish smell.

"Where did you get it?" he asked hoarsely.

Fionnbharr laughed, pleased with himself. "I thought you'd be impressed," he said. "I've been to Rome since I saw you last, and I brought it back. Finer than anything in Erin, wouldn't you say?"

It was not a tactful question to ask a man who spent all his spare time making books, but Columba wasn't paying attention. Something terrible was happening to him. As he looked at the book, all his peace and happiness drained away and was replaced by a passion of greed and jealousy that made him feel sick. He was a monk. He was not allowed to have personal possessions. Yet now he wanted Fionnbharr's book with a desperate longing. Not as a gift for one of his monasteries. Not even to place in his own dear church at Derry. But for himself.

"Very fine," he muttered, as he hurried away. "I congratulate you."

Columba didn't sleep well that night. Tossing on his hard, narrow bed, he was tempted as he had not been for years. He wanted to steal the book. He wanted to use his power to paralyse Fionnbharr and his monks until he was far away. He wanted to burn the book, so that if he couldn't have it, no-one else could either. Of course, deep down he knew that he could not, would not, do any of these wicked things. He was horrified that he could even think about them. The book belonged to Fionnbharr, and that was that—or that was almost that. Columba refused to give up altogether. By the time dawn broke, he had made a plan.

"We're not moving on today," he said abruptly

to Bearchán, who was cheerfully packing their bag before breakfast so that they would lose no time afterwards. "I've decided to stay here for a while."

Bearchán's eyebrows shot up in astonishment, and disappeared under his fair fringe. Columba was always in a hurry when they were headed towards Derry. At one time Bearchán would have started to ask questions, but he was a monk now, and slowly learning obedience. So he said, "Yes, father," and quietly unpacked the bag again.

"He's up to something," said Lua, when Columba had gone over to the dining-hall for breakfast. Lua admired Columba, but he thought he was as wily as a fox. "I wonder what it is?"

"Well, you'll just have to wonder," replied Bearchán, laughing. "He's not likely to confide in us."

Lua kept his keen blue eye on Columba all day, but he could see nothing suspicious in his behaviour. Had he not been such a sound sleeper, however, he would have seen something that night.

When all the monks were asleep, and dawn was a streak of duck-egg blue on the eastern sky, Columba rose stealthily from his bed. Slipping out of the guesthouse, he glided like a long shadow across the grass to the church. There he lit a lamp, pulled out paper, pens and inkhorns that he had hidden behind the ambry, and lifted Fionnbharr's book onto the reading-desk. Placing another desk and a stool beside it, Columba laid out his tools, and positioned the lamp. Then he smoothed his paper, and dipped his pen. "Blessed" was the first word: initial *B*. Columba sketched it in, then peered at the *B* in Fionnbharr's book; he wanted to copy, with perfect accuracy, the wreath of vine-leaves that twisted around it.

It took Columba six nights to copy the whole book. No-one suspected what he was doing, and he told no-one. He knew it was the best copy he had ever made, and that made him happy in a fierce, triumphant way. But his peace of mind was gone. He knew he was deceiving Fionnbharr, who was delighted that he was staying, and treating him as an honoured guest. Yet when his conscience told him he was doing wrong, he excused himself easily. It was Fionnbharr's own fault, he told himself. Fionnbharr had no right to possess anything so beautiful. Fionnbharr should have made him a present of the book, because he was a prince, and Fionnbharr a man of no importance at all. His hard-won humility was gone. Pride and anger were souring and warping Columba, who for ten years had been the happiest man in Erin.

At dawn on Thursday morning, a week after his arrival at Moville, Columba put the finishing touches to his copy of Fionnbharr's book. As the pale morning light strengthened and the glow of the little lamp died, he put the book from Rome back in the ambry, and stood admiring his own. As he waited for the ink to dry on the last page, he planned his departure. He would hide the sheets of parchment under his cloak, and carry them over to the guesthouse. He would wake Lua and Bearchán, and before anyone was about they would be on their way. Once he was back at Derry he would arrange for a fine leather binding to be made for his book...Columba was so deep in thought that he did not hear the church door open, nor the soft tread of sandalled feet over the beaten earth floor.

"What are you doing, my son?"

At the sound of Fionnbharr's voice, Columba jumped like a guilty child. Cursing his ill luck, he whipped round, and saw the old abbot standing by the ambry. He was staring at Columba's book, and as the truth dawned on him, a bright flush stained his thin cheeks. When he raised his brown eyes, Columba shrank from the hurt, reproach and fury he saw in them.

"How dare you?" cried Fionnbharr. "You, who are supposed to be my friend! I have welcomed you and housed you, and you have repaid me by creeping into my church by night, stealing my book, ch-cheating me—"

He was stuttering with rage. Columba opened his mouth to justify himself, to say that copying wasn't stealing, but before he could say more than "Look, father—" Fionnbharr was off again.

"You should be ashamed of yourself," he said wrathfully. "A man of God, behaving like a common thief! But you won't get away with it. The book is mine, so the copy is mine too. Leave it where it is, and get out of here. I never want to see you again."

Columba stared at the old man in astonishment. Fionnbharr had always seemed so gentle, so self-controlled. For the first time, Columba realised that the book was as precious to Fionnbharr as it was to him. But he had been accused of stealing, and he wasn't going to back down now.

"Don't be ridiculous," he said haughtily. "The copy is mine. I made it, and I shall keep it. I'm surprised to find you so unreasonable."

He began to roll the pages up and to tie a thong around the bundle. Fionnbharr watched him bitterly.

"And I am surprised to find you so dishonourable," he said. "But don't think you've heard the last of this. I shall go to the king. He will make sure that I keep what is mine by right."

The word "dishonourable" cut Columba to the heart. Tears rose in his eyes. But he made himself laugh scornfully. "Aodh is my cousin," he said icily. "I doubt that you will find favour with him."

Suddenly, Fionnbharr's anger seemed to drain out of him. When he answered, his voice was as cold as Columba's.

"I am not speaking of Aodh," he said. "Aodh is only a king in Ulster, and this matter is too important to be settled by him. I shall take my grievance to Diarmaid mac Cearúill. The High King of Erin will decide between us. We shall meet at Tara, Columba."

9

Columba of the Battle

It was suffocatingly hot in the great hall. Smoke from the fire on the central hearth, unable to escape through the poorly ventilated walls and roof, hung like a droopy blue blanket below the thatch. The flame of torches, pushed into iron brackets around the walls, raised the temperature even higher, and the stink of sweating, unwashed bodies, dog excrement and stale food was revolting. Columba, who spent most of his life out of doors, was disgusted. His eyes smarted in the peat-reek, and his nose wrinkled fastidiously as the smell invaded his nostrils. It was typical of Diarmaid mac Cearúill, he thought contemptuously, that he had turned the great hall at Tara of the Kings into a filthy sty.

Columba had arrived at Tara that afternoon, summoned by Diarmaid to answer the complaint of Abbot Fionnbharr that he had, by making a copy in secret, stolen the abbot's precious book. He had considered not turning up. The charge was ridiculous, and not worth wasting time over. But it would, he knew, be foolish publicly to snub the High King. Columba hated Diarmaid, who called himself a Christian king but had several wives and surrounded himself with druids, magicians of the old heathen religion. He had even dared to slay a young prince who was under Columba's protection at the time.

Still, it would not be prudent to offend him. Diarmaid had given Columba land for monasteries, and protection for his monks. If he wanted to, he could withdraw these favours and make it difficult for Columba to work in his territory. So, very unwillingly, Columba had decided to come.

He had brought the book with him, as he had been ordered to do. Now it lay on a small table between his chair and the chair where Fionnbharr sat, carefully avoiding Columba's eye. He had been in the courtyard when Columba arrived, looking tired and shrunken after his long journey, a white-haired old man in a grey dress, who reminded Columba painfully of Cruithneachán. For a wild moment he had wanted to run to him, to beg his forgiveness, give him the book and be friends again. But the terrible word "dishonourable" was between them. Columba hardened his heart.

Now they were facing Diarmaid, a dark, thick-necked lout in a stained tunic, with a gold circlet embedded in his bushy hair. He had the kind of red skin that made Columba think of meat. He sat on a throne, on a platform, surrounded by his druids. Columba detested the chief druid, Beag, even more than he did his master. The back of the hall was packed with Diarmaid's kinsmen, nobles, and servants, eager for an unusual entertainment. Columba caught Diarmaid's sneering eye, and looked away again.

Fionnbharr was invited to speak first. Nervously, but with rising indignation, he told his story. He stressed that it was he who had taught Columba the art of book-making long ago, then went on to tell how he had given his old pupil hospitality and shared with him the beauty of the psalter from Rome. He was almost sobbing as he recounted how he had been repaid with dishonesty and treachery. "For if Columba did not know that he was doing wrong," he concluded in his old, high voice, "why did he creep into my church at dead of night, and do in the dark what he dared not do by the light of day?"

A murmur of agreement ran round the hall. Columba sensed sympathy for the aged man, and hostility to himself. He was also disturbed by the question, which was just.

"Would you care to answer Abbot Fionnbharr, Abbot Columba?" enquired Diarmaid, with false politeness and an unpleasant smile. He was enjoying this.

Columba shrugged his shoulders. He could not prevent distaste from showing on his long, aristocratic face. "Certainly not," he snapped. "Abbot Fionnbharr's claim is absurd. I made the copy, and it belongs to me."

"Very well," nodded Diarmaid. Turning, he beckoned to his nine druids. They gathered round him importantly in their yellow robes. Columba watched them, loathing their wagging heads, each with a leaf-shaped bald patch running from brow to crown, like a mockery of the monks' own tonsure. There was much whispering, and some sniggering, before all the druids except Beag withdrew. He and Diarmaid conferred a little longer, then Beag too stood back, with a gleeful smile on his lips. Diarmaid asked the two abbots to step forward. "We have decided," he announced. "To every cow belongs her calf. To every book belongs its little book. Columba's copy belongs to you, Abbot Fionnbharr. Take it with you." Then King Diarmaid smiled.

It was the smile that did it—mocking, triumphant, delighted at Columba's defeat. A red hood of rage seemed to descend over Columba's eyes. He threw back his head, shook his fist, and uttered a loud cry. "May you be cursed, Diarmaid mac Cearúill! This is an unjust judgement, and I shall have my revenge!"

Columba turned on his heel. The crowd divided in front of him as he swept down the great hall, as once the Red Sea had parted to let Moses pass. As he thrust open the door, a great gust of icy night air blew past him through the hall, making the torches flicker and chilling the sweating bodies of those within. Even the king shivered. Silence fell.

Now madness seized Columba. Riding the grey horse King Aodh had lent him, he flung himself into the north, thinking only of revenge. In his pain at the loss of the book and of his humiliation by Diarmaid, a man he despised, he forgot all the lessons of love and humility that Cruithneachán and Mobhí had taught him. He forgot the years when he had walked with God and been happy. Whipping the poor horse on through storm and flood, he swore to get even with Diarmaid mac Cearúill, who disgraced the throne of Tara of the Kings. Bitterly Columba blamed his parents, who had given him to the church without his permission, and so taken away his chance to be elected High King of Erin. All his proud belief that he served a higher king than Diarmaid evaporated, and he was a prince of this world, throttled with rage because another prince had got the better of him. As he crossed the Búir, where once he had knelt to pray, Columba had forgotten God.

As usual, King Aodh received him with honour, and listened to his request, stroking his golden beard. "Declare war on Diarmaid?" he repeated thoughtfully. "Lead the northern Uí Néill against the High King of Erin? That's asking a lot, Columba. He's my cousin, after all."

"And I am his cousin, and you are my cousin," pointed out Columba impatiently. "What has that to do with anything? The man's a villain. He slew Prince Curnán, who was under my protection, and he's an enemy of the church, for all that he calls himself a Christian. He has taken part in filthy heathen practices, and as for those druids ..."

Aodh nodded. He too had heard tales of heathen rites at Tara of the Kings, of a white mare slaughtered, sliced up, and boiled, and of the High King eating its flesh. He found this as repugnant as Columba did, but he would not go to war for that. On the other hand, Aodh was an ambitious man. Defeat for Diarmaid could mean more land, and more power for himself, and Columba was providing him with a fine excuse to fight.

"Go to your cousins of the tribe of Cinéal Conaill," he said. "Go to the King of Connacht. If you can persuade them to join us, I shall lead my army against Diarmaid. God knows, I have no liking for the man."

The grey horse was exhausted. Changing him for a black mare, Columba spurred away into the west.

On a winter day, when a dust of snow blew over the hills, and the sun hung low and red over Benbulbin, the armies of the kings of Ulster and Connacht met the army of Diarmaid, High King of Erin, on the field of Cúil Dreimhne. From morning until afternoon the battle raged. First the kings and princes in their chariots, then the horsemen, then the foot-soldiers hurled themselves into the fight, hacking furiously at one another with their iron swords. Terrible war-cries mingled with the shrill whinnying of the horses and the screams of the wounded. War-horns bellowed like angry bulls, and the echoes boomed from the crags of Benbulbin. Round the fringes of the battlefield prowled Diarmaid's yellow-robed druids, cursing and taunting, chanting magic spells, praying to their dark gods for victory. But Columba stood alone on a high rock, calling loudly to God to strike down his enemies, regretting only that he had never learnt the skills of war.

By noon, the armies of Ulster and Connacht were getting the upper hand. Three hours later it was all over. As the sun went down into a fiery bed, Diarmaid threw down his shield, turned, and drove his chariot from the field. The remnant of his army followed, hanging their heads in defeat. Then, as the cheering, singing survivors of the victorious side grouped around their kings and withdrew to their camp, Columba knew a moment—his last—of sheer, unpitying triumph. Throwing up his arms, he thanked God for this victory and for the humiliation of his enemy. He rejoiced that Diarmaid had not died, but lived to experience despair.

Then, as he prepared to leave his high place and go off to congratulate King Aodh at his camp, something unexpected happened. Down on the field of blood, where the dead and the dying lay, Columba saw movement, and heard voices raised in prayer. As if waking from a dream, he started, and stared. In the half-light of the dying winter day, monks were walking among the recumbent figures, stooping to close the eyes of the dead, kneeling to comfort the dying, raising the wounded to pour water down their parched throats. Columba recognised them. They were brothers from the monastery he himself had founded at nearby Drumcliff. They had waited, as they knew they must, until the men of war had done their worst, and now they had come to perform the tasks that fell to the men of peace.

Shame swept over Columba, and in his head he heard a voice speaking words that Cruithneachán had taught him when he was a little boy. *What doth the Lord require of thee, but to do justly, and to love mercy, and to walk humbly with thy God?*

With tears running down his face, Columba walked down from the rock, and joined his monks on the field of Cúil Dreimhne.

10

Journey

"But what am I to do?" Columba groaned.

The oak leaves about his head were at their freshest and frilliest, and the sun was drawing shifting patterns on the mossy floor of the grove where he was walking with Ciarán. But Columba, who loved spring, was too sick at heart to notice. Ciarán, who had come to Derry to visit Columba and try to comfort him, looked anxiously at his old friend. He had never seen him like this: round-shouldered, pale, and hollow-eyed. He was a poor shadow of the cocksure, domineering Columba whom Ciarán was used to, and the contrast was alarming.

"Since you ask me," said Ciarán, "I think it's time you thought seriously about that pilgrimage you used to be so keen on. A new start, you know. Get out of Erin, at least until the rumpus dies down."

Columba groaned again. He had never felt less like going on pilgrimage in his life. But he knew that Ciarán was right.

The last few months had been terrible. Three thousand men had died at the battle of Cúil Dreimhne, and as many again were badly wounded. Wives were left widows, mothers childless, children fatherless. Men who had lost an arm or a leg, or sustained a bad head wound, would never be able to work again. Beggars sat reproachfully by the wayside, and all over Erin, people looked for someone to blame. They blamed Columba. But not more than he blamed himself.

Bitterly Columba recalled the warnings he had received, from Cruithneachán, from Finnian of Clonard, from Mobhí Cláiríneach, that his temper was dangerous. Bitterly he remembered his own belief that if he misused the power God had given him he could destroy. He had had nightmares for years about the man he had struck down in the plain of Meath, but at least that man had been evil. This time, by losing his temper and using his power to persuade Aodh to go to war, he had caused the death of innocent men, as surely as if he had felled them one by one. He had not lived up to his name.

Ciarán took a different view. "Aodh and his allies were glad of an excuse to go to war," he said. "All kings think about is power, and getting more land. Your book only gave them the excuse they wanted—as I said at the synod last month, if you remember."

Columba didn't remember. He had only one memory of the synod, a meeting of the most important bishops and abbots at Tailte, in Meath, which had been called to discuss his role in the battle against the High King. It was that Fionnbharr had spoken in his defence.

"I am much to blame in this matter," the old man had said. "By my pride and greed, I caused Columba to do what he did. If you are going to drive Columba out of the church, you had better drive me out too."

Apart from the pain of that moment, Columba remembered only the misery of sitting in the centre of their circle, like a criminal, wounded as much by the sympathetic glances of his friends as by the hostile stares of his enemies.

In the end, they had decided not to drive him from the church. Breandán, an old friend from his student days at Clonard, had risen to his feet and told the synod how a messenger from God had appeared to him in a vision and told him that Columba was still intended by God to be a leader of his people. Visions were taken seriously. Columba was reprieved, but not, by everybody, forgiven. He did not need Ciarán to tell him that it would be wise to leave Erin for a while.

"Where shall I go?" he asked.

"To Albain," Ciarán told him without hesitation. "Do you remember Finnian's dream about the two moons? Yours shone over both Erin and Albain. And there was some mention of Albain in a vision your mother had before you were born, if I remember rightly."

Columba sighed. Other people's dreams and visions seemed so meaningless to him now. How could he be a leader of God's people? He had turned away from God when he stormed out of the great hall at Tara of the Kings, and now, he believed, God had turned away from him.

Still, once he had taken a decision, life became easier for Columba. He was a man of action, and there was much to do. The pain he felt at the prospect of leaving Erin was great, but he reminded himself that he had behaved disgracefully, and deserved punishment. Perhaps one day, when he had been punished enough, he might come back to Erin again.

Columba did not intend to travel alone. Twelve other monks would go with him. Just as once he had asked Aodh for land to build his first monastery in Erin, now he must ask another king for a place to build his first monastery in Albain, that mysterious land whose mountains could be seen, hazily blue, from the coast of Erin on a clear day.

This did not prove as difficult as Columba had feared. Some years before, kinsmen of his had crossed the sea and settled on the west coast of Albain. These people called their new home Dál Riada, after the district in Ulster from which they came. The king of Dál Riada in Albain was another of Columba's royal cousins; his name was Conall. So Columba sent a message over the sea to Conall, and after many days an answer came. "Choose an island off the coast of my kingdom and build your monastery there. You will be under my protection, and may travel safely through my lands."

Columba was pleased, although it wasn't really Conall's lands that interested him. The Dál Riadans were already Christian. Columba had his eye on the great heathen kingdom of the Picts that lay beyond.

Columba ordered a curach to be built, a sea-going craft with a sail, and a hull covered with stretched hides. It had to be large enough to carry thirteen monks and their provisions across a hundred miles of open sea. After he had given his instructions to the shipbuilder at Derry, Columba went off to pay farewell visits to his monasteries in Leinster. On his return he went to Moville, to make his peace with Fionnbharr and to thank him for his support at the synod of Tailte. Their quarrel made up, he went on to Gartan, where he had been born and where his widowed mother, Eithne, still lived.

Eithne had heard what had happened at Tailte, and she was absolutely furious—furious that her princely son had been put on trial, furious that not everyone seemed to think him as marvellous as she did, and furious that he was going from Erin and leaving her behind.

"I won't see you," she complained, "from one year's end to the next, and I do so look forward to your visits." Then she gave him a sly, speculative look. "I've had an idea," she said.

Columba watched her cautiously across the hearth in her room, where they were sitting together after supper. He saw the gleam in her dark eye, and wondered what she was up to.

"I suppose you're going to tell me what it is," he said evenly.

Eithne smiled. "I think I'll come with you," she said. "I could be your housekeeper, and help you keep your monks in order. I'm sure many things in a monastery would benefit from a woman's touch."

Columba stared at her incredulously for a moment, then he began to laugh. He laughed until the tears ran down his cheeks, and his sides ached. It was the first good laugh he had had for a very long time.

But, "No, no, no," he said, when at last he could speak again.

Eithne sighed, and tutted impatiently over the stupidity of men. But when Columba left her next morning, she said to him seriously, "I do mean it, you know. I refuse to end my days here in your brother's house, an old crone whom nobody wants, mumbling beside the fire. When you have a place for me, send me word, and I shall come."

This time Columba saw the misery in her eyes, and he did not laugh.

At dawn on a clear May morning in the year 563 the curach of Columba left its moorings at Derry, and as the morning light strengthened it slipped down Lough Foyle towards the sea. Leaving it to others to handle the ship, Columba stood in the bows, seeing the green shores fragmented through his tears. In the evening, as the sun set, he scrambled back over his companions to the stern, to watch the coastline of Erin draw back and merge into the night. He knew that he was torturing himself, but he couldn't help it.

By the next morning he was feeling better. The leaving was over, and he began to feel an interest in what lay ahead. Only occasionally that day did he look back at the blue line drawn on the western horizon. Another blue line, which came and went elusively as the clouds shifted in the east, now claimed his attention. Driven by a strong wind, the curach leaped forward over the waves, carrying Columba and his twelve chosen monks towards the shore of Dál Riada.

When night came, the younger monks shivered with fright, but Columba loved the black sky with its scatter of stars and the slapping of the invisible waves against the side of the ship. For the first time since the battle at Cúil Dreimhne, Columba was able to pray. "*O ye stars of Heaven, bless ye the Lord, praise him, and magnify him for ever. O ye nights and days, bless ye the Lord...*" He was not afraid.

On the morning of the fifth day, Columba was awakened by Diarmaid, the young monk who was to be his friend and companion for the rest of his life. "Father Columba, wake up! Come and see!"

Columba sat up, groaning a little at the pain of

his cramped limbs. But when he saw the cheery, eager young face, he smiled back. "What is it?" he asked.

"Land," Diarmaid replied.

And so it was. When he stood up, Columba saw distant mountains, towering purple through the mist. Nearer to hand, pale green islands floated on the sea.

11

Cúl le hÉirinn

"I don't know about the rest of you," said Eochaidh, "but I'm tired. I'm beginning to think I'll spend the rest of my days sailing round islands, trying to find one you can't see Erin from."

"And supposing there isn't one you can't see Erin from?" said Feachtnach, widening his eyes comically. "What then, brothers?"

"Problems, problems," said Ros.

The young monks giggled, and even the older ones, usually so stern and so quick to silence mirth, smiled into their beards. It did have a funny side. This was the fifth island they had visited. Here they were again, huddled on the shingle in the lee of the curach, sheltering from the biting wind, while the long, lean figure of their abbot strode away from them, up over rock and heather to the highest point of the island. They watched him turn there and stand like a statue, staring keenly out to sea. Unfortunately—in a way—the air was as clear as glass. Then he began to lope down again, covering the grass quickly with his long, athletic steps.

"He could see it," moaned Eochaidh. "Earnán, couldn't you reason with him?"

Earnán, the oldest and greyest of the monks, gave young Eochaidh a withering look. "Listen," he said. "I may be his uncle, but he's my abbot, and I'm as bound to obey him as you are. Anyway, you can't reason with him. Everybody knows that."

Everybody did. Five minutes later, Columba had reached the shore, and they were pushing the curach into the water again. Feachtnach and Scannal raised the sail, and soon the fifth island was falling away astern, gold and green in the sunlight.

Columba looked at the carefully expressionless faces of his companions with a mixture of amusement and sympathy. He knew what they felt and what they were saying behind his back. Of course he didn't have to explain his actions to them, and that was just as well. They thought he was being awkward, but they didn't know the terrible weight of the guilt he carried. The truth was that if he settled on an island from which he could see the smudgy line that was the Antrim coast, he would never be able to put the past behind him. Guilt, love and longing would haunt him for evermore. He must turn away from Erin, and not be able to look back.

But his monks were exhausted, and his troubles were not theirs.

"I'm sorry, brothers," he said. "I do want to sail a little further north. But I promise that even if the next island doesn't suit me, we'll stay there for a few days. I can see that you all need some rest."

"Thank you, father," the monks dutifully replied.

From the sea, the sixth island looked much like the others they had visited, low and green, its shoreline defined by sea-worn, seaweedy rocks. As the curach entered a bay and was coaxed by the tide towards the beach, the brothers saw a tumble of subtly coloured rock on one side. On the other there was a sweep of sandy turf and a scattering of sea pinks and clover. The clear sky that had favoured them ever since they left Erin arched above; if Columba couldn't see the coast of Erin on such a day, he could be sure that he never would. Before the curach beached he was over the side, his sandalled feet splashing through the ripples as he sped eagerly ashore.

"Wait here," he shouted over his shoulder, then he was off, scrambling up over the rocks, appearing and disappearing among the small, grassy ravines above.

The brothers hauled the curach above the tide-line and sat down in the sand. The little bay was sheltered from the wind, and there was welcome warmth in the sun.

"I like it here," said Griollán, picking up a smooth red pebble and admiring it in his palm.

"Don't get too settled," warned Scannal, and everybody laughed.

Columba seemed to be gone for longer than

usual. The sun began to sink behind the rocks, and in the shadow it was cold. The monks looked at one another, uncertain whether their abbot's absence augured well or ill. But when eventually the tall figure of Columba reappeared, somehow they knew before he reached them what decision he had made.

"We stay here," confirmed Columba. "Unload our provisions, and I'll lead you to a sheltered place, where we'll camp tonight. Tomorrow we shall bury the curach in the sand." He looked round the ring of startled, silently questioning faces. "There will be no going back," he explained.

It took all of the next day to bury the curach, using spades Columba had brought, concealed below the rowing-benches. As Ros said sourly, he had thought of everything. That night the brothers again slept in a grassy hollow among the rocks, lulled by the rhythmic splash of small waves coming to shore. The wind had dropped just after their arrival. Columba said rather loftily that he didn't need it any more.

On the morning of the third day, Columba ordered them to pack up what was left of the provisions and to shoulder the bags of seed corn, tools, woollen cloth and books that they had brought with them.

"We'll go further north on the island today," he said, "and look for a good place to plant our monastery." He caught the woeful eye of Scannal, who was staggering under an enormous sack of seed, and burst out laughing. "Cheer up, brother," he said. "It's a very small island. You won't have more than a couple of miles to walk."

He set off at a great pace, striding and leaping among the rocks. The brothers followed as best they could.

It would seem strange to them afterwards that they had not considered the possibility that there might already be people on the island. Probably it was because they had not seen another human being since they sailed out of Lough Foyle many days before. And the islands where they had landed had been so isolated, apparently possessed by puffins, solan geese, and grey seals lazing on the skerries in the sun. So when Columba's little procession descended from the rocks into the pleasant green plain that belted the island from side to side, the brothers—and none more than Columba—were astonished to see, away among the waves of grass, two tall, robed figures hurrying towards them.

"Who are these funny folk?" enquired Griollán.

"Trouble?" wondered Feachtnach.

"They look like monks," said Cofach, who had a habit of stating the obvious. His friends laughed.

"Be silent, all of you," thundered Columba suddenly. There was a holiday spirit among the brothers that was beginning to get out of hand. "Hold your peace. I'll handle this," he added more quietly, seeing their disconsolate faces.

Columba drew apart from the monks, who set down their burdens and stood in a subdued little huddle, watching. The two strangers came closer, wading through long grass in their grey woollen robes. They were bearded and tonsured like monks, and as they approached Columba, each sketched the sign of the Cross in front of him. But it was obvious from their sour expressions that they had not come with words of welcome.

"Greetings. I am Dónall," said the younger of the two, curtly.

"And I am Dallán," said the elder, gruff and snappish. "We are bishops. We would, of course, like to welcome you to our island of Í, but we fear you have made a mistake."

"Indeed," replied Columba, narrowing his eyes, and wrinkling his nose as if there were a bad smell under it. "And what mistake have I made?"

The two men looked pointedly at the little group of monks, standing surrounded by their bags and boxes.

"It appears," said the one who called himself Dónall, rudely, "that you may be thinking of staying."

"Which is out of the question," cut in the one called Dallán, before Columba could reply. "This is our island and we don't want strangers interfering with our work here. You have a boat, presumably. Let us escort you to it, and—" He caught Columba's bleak grey eye, and the glib words faded on his lips. He looked away, shuffling his feet.

Columba observed the two men closely, taking his time, making them nervous. Although they wore the normal monks' dress of habit and sandals, and were correctly tonsured, he thought he had never seen less likely bishops in his life. Monks might have their faults, but at least they could look you in the eye. These shifty, impudent fellows reminded him of—druids. Of course! The hated face of Beag, King Diarmaid mac Cearúill's chief druid, rose in Columba's memory, and he knew these creatures for what they were. No wonder they wanted him off the island!

Columba was furious. Stepping forward, he shot out both hands, grabbed the impostors by the necks of their habits, and lifted them right off the ground.

"Rats!" he cried, throwing them from him in disgust. "Cursed druids! Servants of Satan! I am Columba, servant of the true God, and it is not I who shall need a boat this day. Get you gone! And if I ever see you on my island again, I swear I shall use the power my God gives me to deal with you as you deserve!"

It was very satisfying to see the druids jumping through the grass, tripping over their skirts and falling on their faces in their haste to get away from Columba. And in the afternoon, when they had trudged down over sweetly scented turf to the eastern shore, the brothers saw the false bishops in a tiny curach, paddling frantically away across the sound. The island of Í was Columba's.

During the long, golden summer that followed, Columba and his monks camped on the island while they built a new monastery on its sheltered eastern shore. King Conall proved a good friend to them. After Columba had visited him at his fort of Dunadd, on the mainland, ships crossed to Í carrying wattles, timber, sheep, cattle, poultry, and enough barley to see them through the coming winter and spring. By the autumn the ráth was fenced, church, barn and byre built, and a mill by a stream that flowed out of a small loch nearby. The seed corn was stored, and fields marked out, ready for planting the following year.

The brothers built their cells around the church, but Columba built his apart, on a little rise overlooking the narrow sound and the greater island of Mull. In it he put a desk, a stool, and an ambry for his books and writing materials. But now, and for the rest of his life, he slept on the beaten earth floor, with a stone as his pillow. Sleep, he thought, was a waste of time, and he trained himself to do without it.

Rising long before dawn, Columba would go down to the shore and sit in the sand. Listening to the voices of the sea, he sang his psalms into the night, blessing the Lord who stretched out the heavens like a curtain, who made the clouds his chariot, who walked upon the wings of the wind.

At daybreak, when dove-grey light began to seep across the water, Columba would go walking, covering the tiny island with his long, easy steps.

There were no rustling oak-groves here, only rocks and brittle turf, and the salt breath of the wind from the sea. But there was white sand, and pebbles like jewels, gleaming white, green and red as the tide washed over them. There were seals, and oystercatchers, and flowers growing in the crevices of the rock: thrift, yellow irises, and sea milkwort. Columba would never forget Derry, nor cease to long for the land of his birth, but he was beginning to love Í.

One late summer evening, Columba drew his desk and stool to the door of his cell, and wrote a poem, the first he had composed since leaving Erin.

> Delightful would it be to me to be
>> On the pinnacle of a rock...
> That I might hear the thunder of the
>> crowding waves
>> Upon the rocks;
> That I might hear the roar by the side of
>> the church
>> Of the surrounding sea;
> That I might see its noble flocks
>> Over the watery ocean;
> That I might see the sea-monsters,
>> The greatest of all wonders;
> That I might see its ebb and flood
>> In their career;
> That my mystical name might be, I say,
>> Cúl le hÉirinn...

Cúl le hÉirinn: back turned to Ireland. Turning his back on that dear land was the hardest thing Columba had ever had to do. But now that he had actually done it, he was glad. Here in Í, he would find God again.

12

Through the Great Glen

While winter storms shrieked over Í and black waves thrashed the western shore, ships remained in harbour, and sensible folk stayed at home. From November until the end of March, Columba and his monks were isolated, with nothing to do except to study and to worship God. Despite the hardship of his life, Columba found those days precious. He loved the wild excitement of the storms and the peace that came when the wind dropped, the clouds withdrew, and a wet sun shone wanly over the drenched island. He knew that in the spring new monks would arrive, and once again he would have to face an abbot's problems and responsibilities. Conall had given him permission to found new monasteries anywhere he wished in Dál Riada, and already he had made some tentative plans.

But nothing could be done before spring, and meanwhile he was happy to live quietly on Í, listening for God's voice in the wind, and getting to know the twelve monks whom he had brought from Erin. They were important to him, because he had chosen them as his chief helpers in carrying the Gospel to the heathen people on the mainland. Although he was as strict with them as he was with himself, and occasionally punished them severely if they broke the rules he had made for them, he grew to love them dearly. They were as near as he would ever get to a family of his own.

Then, when the spring leaves in Erin thickened, and on Í tiny anemones unfolded in the grass, the expected curachs came sailing up the sound. An old poem tells of those who came:

His company was forty priests,
Twenty bishops of noble worth;
For the psalm-singing without dispute,
Thirty deacons, fifty youths.

A hundred and fifty-three mouths to feed, a school to establish for fifty students, voyages to be made in search of sites for new monasteries, letters to write—it was as well that Columba didn't need much sleep. There was no time that year to organise the great missionary journey into Pictland on which he had set his heart. But he did make time to solve a problem that had been on his mind for some time.

One morning in July, Columba asked Earnán to walk with him on the shore. "I've been thinking," he said abruptly, "about my mother."

Earnán nodded thoughtfully. Eithne was his sister. "Yes," he said. "I think about her too. I called in at Gartan not long before we sailed, and found her very unhappy. I gather that your brother the chief doesn't exactly make her feel wanted."

"No." Columba was worried, but in spite of himself his lips twitched. "She wanted to come with us," he told Earnán. "She thought she could be our housekeeper, and keep us all in line."

Uncle and nephew grinned. The thought of Eithne organising the brothers was hilarious. At the same time, they knew how desperate she must be even to think of such a thing. Eithne knew the rules of monastic life as well as anyone.

"Of course," Earnán said, "she's been talking about becoming a nun ever since your father died. She has great faith, and that vision she had before you were born showed that she has God's favour. And she's strong. She could bear the hard life."

"Yes," Columba agreed. "That's what I want to talk to you about. I have a plan." Then Columba told Earnán how he had sailed, a few weeks before, to Hinba, an island even smaller than Í, and nearer to the mainland of Dál Riada.

"It's peaceful," he said, "and safe. It's also a perfect place for us to stop off, between Í and the king's fort at Dunadd. I'm going to have a monastery there, and make you its abbot." Columba paused, then added, "What I wondered was—if I brought my mother over, with any of her women who would come with her, and built a small nunnery for her on Hinba—would you take her under your protection?"

Earnán looked gravely at his nephew. "You are my abbot," he pointed out. "You can order me to do anything you like."

Columba nodded. "Of course," he said. "But not this. You'd have to be willing."

"I am willing," Earnán replied.

So Princess Eithne had her wish. The following year she crossed from Erin with her faithful servants, and landed on Hinba. She was glad to leave the noise and commotion of the chief's house and to spend her last days in peace, on a scrap of land protruding from the sea. She loved the quiet of Hinba, the sweet sound of the monastery bell, and the view of misty mountains she had seen in a vision long ago. Like her son, she heard God's voice, shouting in the wind, singing in the waves.

Two years had passed since his arrival on Í, and only now, at the beginning of the third summer, was Columba free enough of other affairs to plan his journey into Pictland. This was the wild, mountainous kingdom to the north and east of Dál Riada, ruled by King Brú mac Maolchon from his fortress at Inverness. On his first visit to Dunadd, Columba had discussed an expedition with King Conall, who had done his best to discourage him.

"Brú himself wouldn't harm you," he told Columba. "You're a prince of the Uí Néill, and he'd respect that. But you couldn't preach the Gospel in Pictland without his permission, and to get that you'd have to travel through the Great Glen to Inverness."

"And?" asked Columba, hiding a smile as he looked at Conall's horrified face.

"And risk being ambushed and murdered before you're out of Loch Linnhe," replied the King bluntly. "Don't imagine that a Pict from the mountains is going to check whether you're a prince before he sticks his spear in your ribs. Why don't you forget it, and work among your own people, here in Dál Riada?"

Columba heard the concern in his voice, and was grateful. But he shook his head. "I've got to go," he said. "It's what I came for, a way of showing I'm sorry for the trouble I caused at home."

Conall had no answer to that. He knew about the trouble Columba had caused at home.

That conversation had taken place two years ago. Now, on a June morning, when lukewarm rain hung like vast cobwebs over the water, Columba and seven wet companions beached their curachs at the head of Loch Linnhe. Baoithín, Columba's second-in-command was there, and Diarmaid, his young attendant. Ros, Feachtnach and Eochaidh had been chosen. Columba's old friends Comhghall and Cainneach had come from Erin to join the expedition, by Columba's special invitation. These two were Irish Picts, who knew the language of the Picts of Albain.

The journey had begun well. They had left Í a week ago, apprehensive, but proud to be taking part. As the days passed their spirits had risen; all but Columba had been fooled by the beautiful weather into imagining that the expedition might, after all, hold no worse dangers than the swarms of midges that danced merrily on the water—and feasted on the brothers. Early this morning, however, it had begun to rain, and mood changed with the weather. Ahead of them was a narrow valley, floored by a shallow, tumbling river and roofed with leaden clouds. Beyond that was the darkness of the Great Glen. As the brothers shouldered the curachs and began to tramp towards its gloomy mouth, depression settled on them—a depression that quickly gave way to fear. Swift and silent as a fever it spread from one to another, and cold hands seemed to touch their hearts.

"Father, I'm frightened," whispered Diarmaid, who was still only a boy.

"Trust God. Say a prayer," advised Columba kindly.

Yet he too felt a prickle of terror. It caught him unawares, because he wasn't easily frightened. For years he had travelled through wild, lonely parts of Erin, and was used to dealing with an occasional wild beast, or a bandit jumping out on him from the bushes. But never in Erin had he felt the lurking menace of this place, where darkly wooded slopes swept up on each side of the river, and above them towered terrible mountains, black and sinister in their cowls of mist. A hawk hung motionless overhead, just below the edge of the cloud.

"What is it about this valley?" demanded Comhghall suddenly. "I'm frightened to death, and I don't even know what I'm frightened of."

"I do," whispered Eochaidh from under his hood. "It's eyes. The trees are full of eyes. We can't see them, but they can see us."

No-one laughed. "Yes," the other monks whispered. "You're right, Eochaidh. That's why it's so scary."

There was silence for a moment, while they looked nervously around. There was no movement in the forest, not even a tremor in the leaves.

"And here's another thing," whispered Ros. "I think ears are listening too."

It took a week to travel the length of the Great Glen, while the soft rain drifted down ceaselessly from the low sky. Where there was deep water they sailed, but they had to carry the curachs for long, weary stretches in between. At night they huddled under rocks, up-ending the boats to provide some shelter. Columba, always the bravest, tried to hearten them with the words of a psalm. "*He shall cover thee with his feathers, and under his wings shalt thou trust ... Thou shalt not be afraid for the terror by night; nor for the arrow that flieth by day ...*"

No arrows flew, but the terror continued by night and day. The brothers saw no-one, but the sense of being watched never left them until at last they set their curachs on the wide, black water of Loch Ness. It was with relief that, as the mist divided, they saw in the distance the great wooden fortress of Brú mac Maolchon, the Pictish king. As Comhghall said, whatever dangers lay ahead, nothing could be as terrible as the journey through the Great Glen. At least now, when hostile eyes looked at the brothers, they would know to whom they belonged.

13

A Trial of Strength

Columba hated the druids. All his life he had
despised them as priests of false gods, and resented
the power they had over kings and princes. But
since King Diarmaid mac Cearúill's chief druid,
Beag, had urged his master to humiliate Columba
in the dispute over the copied book, Columba's
dislike had deepened into real loathing. Now, as
he led his little procession of monks towards the
fortress of Brú mac Maolchon, he was furious to
see in the twilight an opposing procession of yellow-
robed druids. They were hurrying importantly down
the wooden ramp that bridged the ditch in front
of the gates. At their head was an impudent-
looking fellow with a bushy white beard and dark,
malicious eyes. Holding up his staff, he barred
Columba's way, forcing him to halt some way
short of the entrance to the fort. Instantly the
gateway was filled with curious onlookers, tanned,
sturdy men in short tunics, with curly brown hair
and small, pointed beards.

"I am Briochán," said the druid imperiously,

"chief adviser to King Brú. I do not have to ask who you are. Your name is known to us, and we had news of your approach many days ago."

The brothers stole sidelong glances at one another as Comhghall translated his speech. So they had been watched. The hidden eyes in the forest had been real. They waited breathlessly to see how Columba would react to the impertinence in the druid's voice. But for the moment, Columba was keeping his temper.

"Since your knowledge is so great," he replied evenly, "you will also know that I have not come to speak to you but to your master. Kindly escort me to him."

Briochán tutted, pursed his lips, and shook his head in a reproving fashion. "You are too hasty, Columba," he said. "King Brú has not yet decided whether he wants to speak to you. I'm afraid you must wait here until he makes up his mind."

Briochán's smile reminded Columba of Beag's. This man's delight in being insulting and stirring up trouble was exactly the same as the Irish druid's. But still Columba remained cool.

"It is time for our evening service," he said. "We shall hold it now, while we wait for the king to decide to see us." Turning his back on the druids, he motioned to his little group of monks to form a circle, which they did with dignity, taking courage from his example. The psalm for evening was an apt one. *"God is our refuge and strength,"* intoned Columba in his deep, strong voice, *"a very present help in trouble."* The brothers joined in. *"Therefore will not we fear ..."*

The druids were displeased. Briochán tried to interrupt, constantly pushing in to say, "You can't," and, "You're not allowed." His followers, with threatening gestures and chanting of uncouth spells, tried to spoil the monks' singing. But the brothers kept their eyes on Columba's face, and their voices did not falter.

Before long, however, Columba had had enough. All of a sudden, in a voice so loud that it boomed and echoed from the surrounding mountains, he thundered his defiance of the druids and their false gods. The psalm gave him the words. *"The heathen raged, the kingdoms were moved: he uttered his voice, the earth melted ..."* Never had one human being produced such a noise. It wasn't natural. Panic seized the druids. Helter-skelter they scrambled up the ramp and through the gateway, scattering the Picts who had gathered to watch the fun. The heavy gates were slammed shut, and the monks heard the sound of massive bolts being shot inside.

"Oh, dear," began Eochaidh, then caught Columba's eye. The service went on, and ended as if nothing had happened.

As the last words of the evening prayer died away, the brothers looked speculatively at Columba. What, they wondered, would he do next? They were aware of the unseen eyes again, peering from every arrow-slit and aperture in the ugly timber walls of the fortress, while the thunderous outburst of Columba continued to reverberate on the taut air.

They did not have long to wait. Turning on his heel, Columba strode up the ramp to the barred gates. Raising his right hand, he made the sign of the Cross, then, with his staff, he knocked three times. Instantly the bolts inside were violently driven back. The gates flew open of their own accord, and Columba majestically entered the courtyard. Led by Comhghall, the delighted brothers followed.

Everything happened quickly after that. Stunned by the volume of Columba's voice, which he had heard in the innermost room of the fort, and frightened by the power of a man who could open a gate bolted on the inside, King Brú came hurrying out, smiling and holding out his hands. Behind him came his family, his bodyguards, and, looking very put out, his druids.

"Columba, you are very welcome," said Brú mac Maolchon.

Columba and his followers stayed for several weeks with King Brú, and they were well treated. The king had learnt his lesson, and he listened attentively to everything Columba had to say. But it soon became clear to Columba that if Brú and his people were to become Christian, the power of the druids—particularly Briochán—would have to be broken. Brú was still a young man, and Briochán had been his tutor. The king's admiration for

Briochán's paltry magic tricks was immense, and Columba realised that only by using his power to perform greater feats than Briochán's could he hope to influence Brú.

"I don't like it," he said frankly to Comhghall, who shared his quarters. "I hate the idea of using the gift of God to enter into a struggle with a druid. But unless I persuade Brú that my God is greatest, I've little chance of converting his people. I don't know what else to do."

"Then do it," said Comhghall sensibly. "You told me long ago that the old man who brought you up—Cruithneachán, wasn't it?—said that God had given you power, but hadn't told you what to do with it. That means you have to use your own judgement."

Columba nodded. This was the advice he wanted to hear.

Not long afterwards, Feachtnach came to Columba with a worried frown on his thin face.

"Father," he said, "I've just been talking to one of the Picts who works in Briochán's house. He's a good lad, who shows an interest in God's word. He tells me that Briochán has an Irish maidservant. He holds her as a slave, and treats her with abominable cruelty. I was wondering—could you have a word with the king?"

Columba smiled grimly. He knew that this was the opportunity he had been waiting for.

"Leave it to me," he said.

He called Comhghall to come and be his

interpreter. Then he went swiftly to the king's private room, and knocked on the door.

"Enter," said Brú, and Columba went in.

There was a nasty smell. The king was sitting in the half-darkness at a small table, with the ever-present Briochán at his side. Columba found the dirt and disorder of the room unpleasant. He had often thought that Brú had a lot in common with Diarmaid mac Cearúill—and yet, there was something likable about Brú. The young man looked up with uncertain eyes at the tall monk. He secretly admired Columba, but Briochán said such dreadful things about him. It was difficult to know whom to trust.

"Can I help you, Columba?" Brú asked.

Columba was careful always to be polite to the king. He had not forgotten that he and his monks were deep in a hostile land. "Sir," he said, "my business is with your friend, Briochán. Have I your permission to speak to him?"

"With me?" cut in Briochán, thrusting out his bearded chin. "What business can you possibly have with me?"

He spoke as rudely as he dared. Columba resisted the temptation to pick him up and throw him against the wall.

"This business," he told the druid coldly. "I have just been told that in your household you have a servant, a countrywoman of mine, whom you treat cruelly and with disrespect. I demand that you set her free."

Briochán flushed at the peremptory tone. He was not used to being spoken to like this. But he felt on safe ground, convinced that, if necessary, Brú would take his side. "Well, I won't," he said defiantly. "Who are you to give me orders? I bought the stupid girl, and I'll do as I like with her."

He scowled at Columba, but no evil person could ever out-stare Columba's clear grey eyes. Briochán dropped his gaze.

"Very well," said Columba quietly. "But be warned. If you refuse to do as I ask and set the girl free, you shall die before I leave this place."

The king gasped. Briochán tried to laugh, but found he couldn't. He grabbed a glass cup from the table and took a gulp of wine. As Columba and Comhghall left the room they heard a yelp of terror, and the sharp sound of breaking glass.

"Come with me," said Columba to Comhghall and Feachtnach, who was waiting anxiously in the passage outside. Obediently the two monks followed him, out through the filthy courtyard, down to the bank of the River Ness, which curled around the base of the hill where the fortress stood. Passing the muddy, trampled shallows where the cattle drank, Columba led Feachtnach and Comhghall far upstream, to a place where the water ran clear, and small trout darted among emerald weed on the pebbly bottom. Jumping down from the high bank, Columba squatted by the river's edge and picked out a small, round white stone. He showed it to his companions.

"Take a good look at this pebble," he told them. "God will use it to cure many diseases among the Pictish nation."

Comhghall and Feachtnach peered at the ordinary-looking stone, then glanced at each other in astonishment. But before they could think of a reply, the thud of galloping hooves was heard, and two horsemen appeared, spurring their mounts along the top of the bank.

"Just as I expected," said Columba.

"Columba!" cried one of the riders, reining in his horse so suddenly that the poor creature slipped and nearly fell. "I have a message from the king. Briochán is terribly ill. His face is purple, and he can scarcely breathe. If you don't help him he'll choke to death."

"And we're to tell you," shouted the other man, "that Briochán is willing to release the Irish maid. Will you come now, in the king's name, and cure his friend?"

Columba dropped the white pebble into Feachtnach's hand. "Take this stone to the king," he said. "Tell him to put it in a cup of water, and give Briochán the water to drink. If he truly means to keep his promise, he will be healed."

The horsemen wheeled about, and galloped off in the direction of Brú's fortress. Feachtnach and Comhghall hurried excitedly after them. But Columba walked calmly on, further upstream, enjoying the rustle of leaves over his head and the soft chuckle of the river at his feet. It reminded him of the Leannan, beside which he had lived when he was a boy.

Not surprisingly, Briochán was not at all grateful for his cure, since he blamed Columba for making him ill in the first place. He was also furious at the loss of his servant-girl, who lost no time in leaving the district. But the druid had had a bad fright, and was unwilling, while Columba was still Brú's guest, to attack him openly. Brú was deeply impressed by Columba's power, especially when he saw other sick people cured by the holy stone.

"It must be preserved carefully," Brú said. "One day I may need it myself." (This selfish carefulness did him no good. It is recorded that many years later, on the day when Brú was at the point of death, mysteriously the stone could not be found.) Meanwhile, however, he gave Columba permission to preach his Gospel among the Picts. Much to the druids' annoyance, many people were persuaded by the power of Columba's words, and turned away from the dark gods. So Briochán and his followers were, shamefully, delighted when they heard that the son of Bionga and Clóideach, poor peasants who had recently become Christians, was ill and about to die.

The druids hurried gleefully to Bionga's hut, and crowded into the dark, smoky interior, where the little boy lay unconscious on a bed of straw. The poor parents were in tears, but the dreadful Briochán had no pity for their distress.

"It serves you right," he told them venomously. "Our gods are angry, because you have turned away from them. This is your punishment, to know that you are to blame for the death of your son." Laughing unpleasantly, he added, "Come on, then. Let's hear you pray to your new God. Let's see if he will help you."

"He will help them," said a calm voice, which Briochán knew well. A tall figure filled the narrow doorway of the hut. "Get out of here, vile man," said Columba, "and take your friends with you."

Briochán cursed under his breath. How on earth had Columba known where he was? Would he never be rid of this man? Still, experience had made him wary. Angrily he ordered his fellow-druids to leave the hut. They withdrew to a little hill nearby, where they stood glowering and stamping, in their usual fashion.

Columba, who had now mastered enough of the Pictish language to make himself understood, spoke gently to the anguished father and mother.

"Have faith," he said. "You have a God who will never forsake you. Tell me the child's name."

"Fearadhach," Clóideach said. She and Bionga looked desperately into Columba's face, trying to believe, but almost afraid to hope.

Columba knelt beside Fearadhach's still body, and took the small hand in his large one. He remembered a day long ago, in a wood in Erin, when his had been the small hand, and Cruithneachán's the large. That was the day when he had first realised that God had given him power over life and death. Sometimes that power had been a terrible burden, but now he was glad of it, glad that he could give this child back to his parents, and so prove that his God was strong, faithful, and good. Concentrating very hard, he pressed the boy's hand, and touched his head with his long fingers.

"Wake up, Fearadhach," he said. "The sun is shining. You can go out to play now."

14

A Monster, and a Wild Wind

On the day when Columba told King Brú that he must leave at the end of the week, Briochán was the happiest man in Pictland. He was having problems. Every trick he played on Columba had come to grief, and his complaints to the king about Columba were falling on deaf ears. The news of Fearadhach's recovery had spread like wildfire, and Brú's awe at the sight of the healthy boy, skipping at Columba's heels and asking how soon he could come to Í to join the brothers, was as great as everyone else's. Columba's name was on everybody's lips. Since the story of the purple-faced choking fit had leaked out, however, the mention of Briochán's name made people laugh. This angered and frightened the druid. He hoped that when Columba was gone they would all forget and he would get his power back—a vain hope, as it turned out.

Columba intended to leave on Saturday. On Friday he wanted to pay a farewell visit to a village on the opposite bank of the River Ness, at its junction with the great water of the loch. So, very early in the morning, he set off with Baoithín, Diarmaid, and Cainneach, taking one of Brú's servants, Lúna Mochuimín, as a guide.

There was a smell of autumn among the trees. It was only the end of August, but already the frail birches were hung with yellow leaves, and berries were ripening fast on the mountain ash. When the sun had burned a hole in the clouds it would be a golden day, but now the chill morning mist curled like smoke around the hems of the monks' habits and covered their hoods with minute silver beads. As they moved in single file along the river bank, they were in contented mood. Their expedition had been successful, and tomorrow they were going home. As the great mountain-shadowed loch came into view, vast, dark, and unthinkably deep, a slight unease visited them, but it was nothing compared to the terror that had stalked them on their journey north. They thought that kind of terror was gone for good. They were wrong.

As they climbed into the boat that Lúna Mochuimín had borrowed to take them across the river, the monks were aware of some commotion on the other side. Peering through the mist, they could make out a group of men and women on the shore. The sound of wailing, which always meant that someone had died, warned them that a funeral was taking place. When the boat ran ashore on the shingle, Columba was first out, hurrying along the river bank towards the mourners.

The other monks followed, then Lúna, after he had safely beached the boat. When they caught up with Columba, the burial of the dead person was over, and the two gravediggers were levelling the top of the grave with their spades.

"What happened?" Columba was asking, as the wailing died away and the mourners gathered round in respectful silence.

One of the gravediggers, a strong, brown man with grizzled hair and fearful eyes, replied. "Sir," he said, "the dead man was my cousin. Yesterday, when he was swimming across the river, a terrible monster arose from the water and attacked him. His son here"—the man indicated a tear-stained lad of about sixteen—"bravely ran with a hook and pulled his father out. But it was too late. He had been—largely eaten, sir."

A great sob broke from the crowd, and the dead man's son added, "My father was not the first of our people to be killed by this evil monster. The water runs red with blood because of him. He dwells deep in the loch, but sometimes comes right upstream to find his prey. We are all very afraid."

The mourners nodded, and other voices joined in.

"The monster has jaws as wide as a curach, sir."

"And teeth like whetted knives."

"His eyes are like crimson moons."

"And his tail is a snake's, all scaly and green. Never have I seen such a tail."

Diarmaid had gone very pale. His teeth chattered, and, not for the first time, he wished he had never left Erin. There were no snakes there, because St Patrick had banished them long ago. Baoithín and Cainneach did not look much better, but Columba seemed more interested than alarmed.

"Lúna Mochuimín," he said, ignoring his monks, of whom he was not particularly proud at this moment, "you seem a brave fellow. Will you help me rid these poor people of this wicked monster?"

"Gladly, sir," said Lúna firmly. He was Fearadhach's uncle, and he trusted Columba with his life. "What do you want me to do?"

"Do you see that curach on the river bank opposite?" Columba asked. Lúna nodded. "Then throw off your cloak," urged Columba. "Swim across, and bring it back to me."

A gasp, half of admiration, half of horror, arose from the onlookers as Lúna took off his sandals, removed his cloak, and plunged into the water. Then there was complete silence as they watched his brown head bobbing and the triangular rippling made by the frog-like movement of his legs. He was half way across when the monster surfaced.

With a suddenness that caused a stampede of panic from the shore, the great emerald-green serpent reared out of the slow-running water, red eyes glaring, forked tongue darting, fangs bared in a terrible grin. Thrashing his incredible tail so that the water boiled around him, he bore down on Lúna with a bellow that shook the woods and turned the bravest hearts to ice. The smell of his breath tainted the air. Diarmaid fainted. So did Baoithín.

But Columba waded eagerly into the water, and when the monster's slavering jaws were no more than a spear's length from Lúna's bare feet, he made a flamboyant sign of the Cross.

"Monster, hear me!" he cried in a loud, commanding voice. "You shall go no further. Do not touch that man, and leave this river at once!"

The enormous creature stopped so abruptly that his ugly head jerked back, and he rose on his tail to form a towering S-shape on the water. The fiery light of his eyes dimmed, and a long hiss of fear issued between his drawn-back lips. Then, as if he were being pulled backwards by invisible ropes, he reversed swiftly into the middle of the loch, looped, dived, and was gone.

Lúna waded out on the other side, waved to Columba, and went to fetch the curach.

"I have never been so terrified in my life," said Diarmaid to Comhghall that evening. "When I get back to Í, I'm going to crawl into my cell, put a stone across the door, and never come out again. Not ever."

Comhghall laughed. "Nonsense," he said. "You'll tell the story to everyone you meet, with yourself as hero, I shouldn't wonder."

Diarmaid blushed, but didn't contradict him.

Next morning everyone was up early, and there

was much running to and fro. Brú had decided to accompany Columba to the head of Loch Ness. From there, the brothers were to sail down the loch in one of the king's ships. Servants of the king would escort them the length of the Great Glen, carrying the curachs and abundant provisions; it would be a very difficult journey from the terrifying trek north, ten weeks before. Of course where Brú went, his servants, his bodyguards and his druids went too. Briochán could not hide his happiness as he bustled about, organising the king's short excursion. He made such a fuss, anyone might have supposed Brú was going all the way to Í. Every so often the druid flashed Columba a triumphant leer, which Columba, waiting in the courtyard for the king to be ready, ignored. He was in no doubt why Briochán was feeling triumphant, however.

On the day when Columba had announced the end of his visit, Briochán, though longing for him to go, had not been able to resist saying, "I'm sorry, Columba. I'm afraid you can't go on Saturday."

"Indeed?" Columba had replied, coolly.

"Indeed," mimicked Briochán. "I'm going to prove my power to you, once and for all. I'll make the wind unfavourable to your voyage, and a great darkness will wrap itself around you. You'll see."

His silly, pleased face had looked so absurd that Columba had wanted to laugh. But he had made no reply, and the matter had not been mentioned again. Presumably Briochán knew, as Columba did, that he was taking a great risk, but it looked this morning as if his gamble might have paid off. There was rain on the wind, and it was blowing from the south.

It was midday when they reached the meeting of the river and the loch, where Brú's oaken ship rode at its moorings on the dark water. As the procession, with Brú and Columba at its head, passed the scene of yesterday's encounter with the monster, the whole village turned out to join them. So a great crowd was present at the loch-side to watch the departure of the brothers from Í.

Briochán was jubilant. As the procession halted, the wind, which had been boisterous all morning, rose suddenly and alarmingly. Brú's cloak was whipped out straight behind him, and the wide robes of the druids billowed hugely, like yellow tents. The surface of the loch heaved ominously, as black clouds, propelled by the tempest now roaring up the loch, unrolled themselves like a carpet across the sky. There was darkness at noon.

"See, Columba! What did I tell you? You can't leave today!" cried Briochán, capering up from the rear and planting himself in front of Columba and the king. He could not keep the grin off his face. "I forbid it," he added smugly.

Then it began to rain.

It was not a time when people really understood coincidence, but Brú, who formerly would have been amazed at Briochán's ability to raise a storm, was now less convinced of his power. His chief concern was for the safety of his guests.

"Columba, please come back with me," he pleaded, paying no attention to the flapping druid. "You can't go on the loch in weather like this. Stay for a few more days."

Columba smiled at him. "I have to go," he said simply. "But have no fear. The God who brought me here safely will see me safely home."

Then he embraced Brú, and calling to his monks to follow him, he waded through the churning water to the ship.

"Fools! They'll be drowned," growled Briochán, peeved, but hopeful at the same time.

"I think not," replied the king.

Controlling his petrified monks with a warning eye, Columba took his seat in the bows of the violently rocking ship. "Don't be afraid," he soothed the trembling sailors. "My God will protect us. Raise the sail!"

And because there was something about Columba that made you do crazy things when he asked you to, the sailors obeyed. While four of them struggled with the stays, a fifth untied the rope that held the ship to a stake in the water. As the fawn-coloured sail unfurled, the vessel swung out sharply into the loch. But then, to the open-mouthed amazement of the people on shore, it wasn't swept back into the mouth of the river and grounded ignominiously on the shingle. Instead, for perhaps half a minute, the sail puffed out towards the north, while the ship ran swiftly in the opposite direction. And just as Briochán whimpered, "It's not possible," the wind that had been making his robes blow out absurdly behind him veered suddenly round, and blew them out in front. It had the same effect on the sail of the ship, which now puffed out towards the south. A sigh of admiration rose from the onlookers, which was like poison in the druids' ears.

The wind stopped screaming, and blew sensibly. The clouds parted, and the sun looked through. As Columba sailed away down the loch, and Brú turned rather sadly to go home, the villagers drew back into the wood. They wondered whether anyone would ever believe the tales they had to tell, but they knew what they had seen. Columba's God was as powerful as he said. Briochán and his druids were left stamping and cursing on the shore. They had been outsmarted yet again.

15

The Dear Green Place

"Speak not, except on business" was one of the rules Columba had made for his monks. It was supposed to stop idle chatter and gossip, which would distract them from thinking of God. Of course, getting the brothers, especially the younger ones, to keep the rule was a different matter. If he caught them chattering, Columba punished them, but he couldn't be everywhere at once. So he was not at all surprised, a few days after the return to Í of the party from Pictland, to discover that everyone in the monastery had heard their adventures. The story of the Loch Ness monster, and the account of Briochán's choking fit, particularly took the fancy of the brothers.

Columba was mildly annoyed, but he understood. The brothers were Irish, with the Irish love of good tales. Columba knew that as a young monk he wouldn't have been able to resist telling such dramatic stories, which were as good as any he had heard while staying with the bard Geamán long ago.

Besides, while he felt that he must punish those whose behaviour interfered with their duty to God, Columba was aware that he himself was still anything but perfect. Although he lived far away from scenes of battle, the blood of warrior princes still ran hot in his veins. Impatiently he awaited news from Erin about the plotting and fighting going on among the kings, and he frequently offered them advice—or interfered, as he would despairingly tell himself afterwards. And, although he had better control of his temper than in his youth, he could still have tantrums, and behave in a way of which later he was ashamed. For instance, the name "Molua" made him blush every time he thought of it.

Although certainly the most powerful, Columba was not the only Christian abbot working in Albain and looking for sites for new monasteries. One of the others was called Molua. He had already annoyed Columba by settling in Tiree, a large island that provided the monks of Í with much of their corn and which Columba regarded as his property. So Columba was very peeved when, sailing one day to claim the island of Lismore for a new monastery, he saw Molua in another boat, sailing in the same direction. Although normally a placid man, Molua wasn't pleased either. A race began, to see who could land on Lismore first.

It was a grey, breezy day, with the tide running fast. The oarsmen in both boats, loudly encouraged by Molua and Columba, bent keenly to their task. Sweating and grunting, they pulled towards the beach. It was neck and neck, but then, at the last moment, Columba's boat edged ahead.

Molua must have been far too excited to think what he was doing. Grabbing an axe that lay in the bottom of the boat, he chopped off his little finger and threw it onto the beach. It fell, staining the sand with a thin, dark trickle of blood, seconds before Columba's boat ran ashore.

"My flesh and blood have first possession of the island!" cried Molua in triumph. "I bless it, in the name of the Lord!"

Columba was livid. He had been outwitted, and, accustomed as he was to outwitting other people, he didn't like it at all. Instead of being ashamed, or concerned about Molua's injury, he leaped out of his boat, stormed up to the white-haired abbot, and began to curse like a druid.

"May you have alder for your firewood!" hissed Columba spitefully.

"The Lord will make the alder burn pleasantly," Molua assured him.

"May you have jagged ridges for your pathways!" snarled Columba.

"The Lord will smooth them to the feet," Molua replied.

And so it went on. Columba had not, as he groaningly admitted to himself later, behaved at all well. Indeed, set against such loss of self-control on the part of their abbot, a little whispered story-telling by the brothers seemed a small sin. Columba didn't make a fuss.

During the months and years that followedColumba worked tirelessly to establish the Christian religion in Albain, where, he was sure, God had sent him. Most of all he loved to be on Í, reading and praying and copying his books, looking out to sea, listening to the wind. On Í, where he had found God again, he would always be most aware of God's presence. But come spring, he was off again, founding monasteries on Skye, Bute, Eigg, and Mull, and in Lorne and Morvern on the mainland. With the approval of King Brú he travelled safely through Pictland, using his power to heal the sick and to persuade people to believe in his God. He revisited Erin, and was surprised that, when the time came to leave, he sailed for Í with the gladness of one going home. He made friends in all the kingdoms of Albain. One of these was Ruairí Caol, king of Strathclyde, who lived in a fortress high on the rock of Dumbarton, above the river Clyde.

Ruairí had a problem, not uncommon among kings. He was terrified that he would be ambushed and killed by his enemies. He wore padded clothes, and couldn't walk down a passage in his own fortress without twitching, and looking over his shoulder. Ruairí was a nervous wreck.

One day he had a visit from Lúna Mochuimín, who, after his spectacular escape from the monster in Loch Ness, had become a monk. After old Earnán's death, Columba had made Lúna abbot of Hinba. But, like Columba, he travelled about a great deal. Often his journeys took him among the people of Strathclyde, who were called Britons. Calling on King Ruairí, Lúna found him in a terrible state, and felt sorry for him.

"Listen," Lúna said. "You should consult Columba. He has the power of prophecy, and can often foretell what the future will bring. If anyone can set your mind at rest, he can."

Ruairí glanced over his shoulder to make sure no-one was listening. "Will you take a message to him for me?" he asked in a whisper.

"Certainly," Lúna replied.

When Columba received the message from Ruairí, he sat down at once and wrote a reply. "Stop worrying. You will never be delivered into the hands of your enemies, but will die at home, on your own pillow."

When he read these comforting words, Ruairí was overjoyed. He took off his padded coat, stopped looking behind him, and became a happier, more confident man. And when, some time afterwards, he was visited by Ceanntiarna, an important bishop whose church was at nearby Glasgow, Ruairí told him about Columba, and the message that had changed his life.

Ceanntiarna knew that Columba's followers were active in Strathclyde. Although he really thought of the Britons as his people, he was too fine a person to be jealous, or to feel that Columba was trespassing on his territory. Provided that God's word was preached, Ceanntiarna didn't mind too much who did the preaching. It was not surprising that his nickname was "Muinghiú," meaning "beloved friend." Now he smiled at Ruairí.

"It's strange that you should have had a message from Columba," he said, "because I have, too. Perhaps hearing from you put him in mind of me. He wants to visit me. He's coming next month."

"I'm not surprised that you want to meet Ceanntiarna," said Comhghall, who was on one of his frequent visits to Í from his own monastery at Bangor in Down. "Everyone says what a good man he is." He grinned mischievously and added, "It seems his power to make unusual things happen is almost as great as yours."

There was a time when Columba would have bristled at this remark. In his haughty youth he would have disliked the suggestion that anyone else's power could rival his. But now he was growing old, and it was easier to put God's glory before his own. So he returned his old friend's grin, and didn't rise to his bait.

"Are you going to come with me?" he asked.

"I wouldn't miss it for anything," Comhghall replied. "But it isn't only me you'll have to take. Ceanntiarna is an important bishop. You can't go off to meet him looking like an old beggar, with Diarmaid and Baoithín running at your heels. You'll have to have a new cloak, without any holes in it, and take a large company of brothers with you, as befits the abbot of Í."

Columba groaned. "Oh, dear. Will I?" he sighed.

"Well, perhaps you're right. I'll ask Scannal to weave me cloth for a new cloak. How large a company do you suggest?"

"Two hundred would be a suitable number," said Comhghall.

Columba groaned again.

Often, during the days that followed, he wished he had never even thought of going to visit Ceanntiarna. He was used to travelling light, with half a dozen companions at most, and organising an expedition for two hundred gave him headaches. Eventually, however, he was ready, in his new cloak and carrying a beautifully polished wooden staff. It had been made by one of the brothers, lovingly carved like a shepherd's crook to show Columba's importance as abbot of Í. He had trimmed his beard and tidied up what was left of his tonsure; since the hair at the front of his head had thinned, it was hard to tell where bald head ended and tonsure began. At least Comhghall couldn't tease him about this, since his dark curls had vanished long ago.

Curachs lent by King Aodhán of Dál Riada, Conall's successor, arrived to convey the travellers to the mainland, and on a calm August morning two hundred brothers sailed from Í. They did their best to hide their delight at being chosen behind grave, dignified faces, but their barely suppressed excitement seemed like the whirr of invisible insects on the air. Looking back from the leading curach at the long convoy behind, Columba wondered ruefully if he had gone mad.

Once they were ashore, however, he enjoyed the long tramp south under mellow summer skies, the picnic meals, the nights spent under the stars. By sea lochs and brackeny mountains they marched, down from the highlands to the green, wooded banks of the Clyde. Striding along at the head of the column, listening to the brothers singing, Columba could not help imagining himself a king, leading his army—the king he might have been if God had not had other plans.

On the morning of the tenth day, coming to a grassy wedge of land, angled by the Clyde and a pleasant stream that hurried down to meet it, Columba saw ahead of him a village. Not far off were the familiar ráth and woven fence of a monastery. The brothers heard the clear, godly chime of the sanctuary bell, ringing to greet them.

"This is the place," Columba said. "Diarmaid, you and Feachtnach must hurry ahead to the monastery and announce our arrival. Comhghall, help me to get our people organised. I want young brothers in front, older ones in the middle, and those with the greyest hair in the rear."

There was chaos for ten minutes as the brothers scrambled to get into the right order, and Comhghall roared at the youngsters to tie their girdles properly and to straighten their sleeves. The commotion brought out the villagers, who scrambled up to the highest ground to get a good view. Men, women and children, barefoot and in tattered tunics, stood gawping and waiting for the unexpected entertainment to begin. By the time Feachtnach came panting back, with Diarmaid at his heels, everyone, including the audience, was ready.

"Now," said Columba, "we'll sing the song we practised on the way. All together—one, two!"

"The saints shall go from strength to strength. Hallelujah," sang the brothers as the column moved, slow and stately, over the grass.

For a moment there was no response. But then, as Columba's monks approached the monastery, the gate opened, and a similar procession came out to greet them. It was led by Ceanntiarna himself, a broad-shouldered, youngish man of middle height, with wiry fair hair. His robes were so white that Columba couldn't help smiling. It was as well he had taken Comhghall's advice and acquired a new cloak.

Ceanntiarna's monks were singing too. *"How great is the glory of the Lord!"* When the heads of the two columns met, Ceanntiarna held out his hands to Columba, a delighted smile lighting up his round, sun-burnt face.

"Columba," he said warmly, "welcome to Glaschù, to our dear green place. Welcome to you all!"

In the evening, after Columba and Ceanntiarna had walked and talked on the bank of the Molendinar stream, a feast was held. Columba, Ceanntiarna and the most senior brothers shared a table, while the others sat in companies on the grass. A feast was the rarest of treats for monks, whose meals normally consisted of a little fish and some barley bread. Ceanntiarna, to celebrate a great occasion, had provided salmon from the Clyde, eggs, cheese, and apples, and honey for the brothers to spread on their bread. Afterwards, as the setting sun burnished the river, they worshipped God together.

It had been a wonderful day. No-one who was there would ever forget it.

Columba stayed for several days with Ceanntiarna. It was wonderful to talk to an equal, someone who really understood the burdens, joys and disappointments of an abbot trying to convert a heathen land. He was also able for the first time to discuss the strange power that God had given him, because Ceanntiarna had it too. He told Columba how, when he was a child at school, he had brought back to life the pet robin of his teacher, Searbhán, which had been cruelly killed by another boy.

"I remember how astounded I was when its little stiff body began to flutter in my hands," he said. "And then one night when our fire had gone out, and poor old Searbhán was shivering with cold, I picked up a frozen branch and—well, it burst into flames. That was when I knew that God had chosen me. I had no choice in the matter."

"That's been my experience too," agreed Columba. "There were times, when I was younger, when I felt a bit rebellious. But now, I wouldn't want anything to have been different."

On the morning when the brothers from Í were to leave on their homeward journey, everyone felt sad. Columba and Ceanntiarna knew how unlikely it was that they would ever meet again. Columba made Ceanntiarna a present of his staff, made of beech from a Dál Riada forest. In return, Ceanntiarna gave Columba his own staff, made of oak from a grove in Wales, where he had lived for a number of years. Then they hugged each other, and said goodbye.

As Columba led his monks away from the dear green place, the bell that Ceanntiarna had brought home from a pilgrimage to Rome rang out behind the monastery fence. For a long time its sweet, insistent voice followed them on the wind. But at last it faded into silence, as the procession moved steadily downriver, towards the sea.

16

A Visitor from Erin

As the years passed and the evening of his life approached, Columba left the travelling to his younger brothers, and stayed at home on Í. He was always busy, reading and writing, supervising the work of the monastery, receiving guests, planning the future. Still he slept only briefly on the floor of his cell, with a stone for his pillow, and spent most of the night on the shore, praying and reciting psalms. Old age invaded his bones slowly, and it was a surprise to realise one day that he was older now than Cruithneachán had been when they parted on the banks of the Leannan that spring morning long ago.

Like all old people, Columba remembered his childhood clearly, and often he seemed to hear Cruithneachán's voice saying, "But wisdom? Oh, Colm! For you, wisdom will be very hard to attain."

He had been right, Columba knew. It had been a long, hard battle to subdue his fierce temper and to acquire the wisdom that has at its heart love, compassion, and the understanding of another's pain. So many failures, so many tears, so many vows to start again and do better next time! Had he attained wisdom yet? Would Cruithneachán be proud of him now? Sometimes, Columba thought, he got things right. There was the case of Earc, for instance.

Years ago, Columba had got used to the fact that sometimes he had knowledge of what went on without actually seeing events with his physical eyes. It was an aspect of the power God had given him. So, one day he had been aware that a man called Earc had sailed from his home on the island of Colonsay to Mull. Earc was hiding among the sand dunes, across the sound from Í, under a boat that he had camouflaged with hay. During the night, Earc sailed across to a little island where young seals, belonging to the monastery, were reared. When he had killed as many as his boat would hold, he sailed back to his hide-out.

The seals provided the brothers with meat, skins, and oil for their lamps, and Columba could not allow such theft to continue. Calling two of the brothers, he sent them over to Mull to arrest the robber. Taken completely by surprise, Earc gave himself up without a struggle, and an hour later found himself standing in front of Columba. He had heard many tales of the abbot of Í, whose powers were by now legendary; he was terrified, and his legs shook so violently that he could scarcely stand upright.

Columba had been angry about the loss of his

seals. But he knew that God had blessed his island with abundance of good things—cattle, sheep, corn, and fish—while Earc had nothing. As he looked into the robber's unhappy eyes and saw the thinness of his bent, rheumaticky body, Columba's anger evaporated. Intense pity took its place.

"Earc," he said gently, "why do you break God's commandment by stealing other people's property? You know better, don't you?"

Earc nodded dumbly. Of course he knew better, but he was hungry. So were his wife and children, and his old parents.

Columba knew this too. "Listen," he went on. "If you are in want, don't steal. Come and tell us, and we'll supply your needs."

Earc could not believe his ears. Slowly it dawned on him that he was not to be punished. "Abbot Columba," he stuttered. "I—I—that is, thank you."

Columba smiled at him. "I'll have some sheep killed," he said. "You'll have them to take home with you, instead of the seals. And I'll send you more, and a gift of corn from time to time."

Yes, Columba thought, Cruithneachán would have approved—though he might have approved less on a different occasion, when Columba chased another robber into the sea and stood up to his knees in the water, screaming curses and shaking his fist ... To the very end, wisdom was hard to attain.

Sometimes he had a fancy that he would be happy living alone, with only the birds for company. Ever since he had lived in Cruith-neachán's house as a small child he had loved birds, and known their names. Later, he had heard from Geamán the legends of how Cú Chulainn harnessed swans to his chariot, and of the swans in the dream of Aonghas, linked together by silver chains. He had delighted in the tale of the four bright birds that hovered around the head of Aonghas Óg. Indeed, the only bird that Columba hated was the raven, which was sacred to that dark, heathen goddess the Mór-Ríon. Ravens croaked in his nightmares, as they had croaked through the mist on Benbulbin, above the battlefield of Cúil Dreimhne.

Columba knew that he had a bird nickname, "the crane-cleric"; he was never sure whether this was a joke at the expense of his long, thin-necked appearance or a reference to the time when he had saved a poor, bewildered crane from the sea. Once again Columba had seen what was going to happen before it did. For nights he had seen the crane in his dreams, and when he had gone down to the shore to pray he had known it was out there somewhere, storm-tossed and hungry, scarcely strong enough to flap its wings. It troubled him, and one morning he called Scannal to him.

"Brother," he said, "three days from now, on Tuesday morning, I want you to walk to the other side of the island. Sit down on the shore, facing Erin. At nine o'clock you will see a crane drop down exhausted on the beach. The poor bird has been blown all over the ocean by contrary winds, and it will be near to death, so you must treat it tenderly. Take it to a neighbouring shelter, nurse it, and feed it for three days. It will then be recovered and ready to fly away, so you can release it. It will fly back to the pleasant part of Erin where it belongs." He paused, then added, "I'm asking you to take special care of this crane, because it comes from our native place."

Scannal nodded, and said, "Of course, father." He was not in the least surprised, having lived now with Columba for more than thirty years. Nor was he surprised on Tuesday morning when the crane arrived at exactly the time Columba had foretold. He did as Columba had instructed him, thankful that the crane was too tired to protest; it was a big bird, with a very sharp beak. Leaving it comfortable, penned up with food and water, Scannal walked back to the monastery, in time for evening prayers.

Columba met him at the church door. "Scannal, you're back," he said. "God bless you, my son, for your kind attention to this foreign visitor." Not "Did the crane arrive? Did you do as I said?" Scannal wasn't surprised at that either.

For three days he looked after the crane. Then, on the morning of the fourth day, seeing it fully recovered, he let it go.

It was a calm, windless day. The crane took off from the turf roof of the shelter. Up, up into the air it went on its wide, slate-grey wings, circling about Scannal as he stood on the beach.

"Kr-rooh!" it cried. "Kr-r-r-rooh!"

Then it stretched out its long neck, pointed its beak towards Erin, and flew in a straight line out to sea.

17

The Holy Man

*O all ye green things upon the earth, bless ye the
Lord; praise him, and magnify him for ever.*

The last summer days that Columba spent on Í
were as beautiful as the first. From early morning
until evening, when the westering sun shook out
its banners of rose and gold, the island lay serenely
under a peaceable sky. Green and silver waves
swished over the rocks and onto the sand, and the
flowers that Columba loved studded the grass,
pink, yellow, and white. The corn the brothers had
planted in spring ripened early, and May would
have been delightful that year, but for one thing.
Columba was dying. No-one who looked at him
could doubt it, and to the brothers, stricken with
grief and fear, the perfect weather seemed a mockery
of the winter in their hearts.

It was not so for Columba. He was seventy-five
now. Four years had passed since he first had a
vision of angels standing on a rock beyond the
sound, waiting to escort him to Paradise. He had

yearned to go with them, but had felt that the prayers of his monks were hindering his departure. So, sadly, he had resigned himself to a longer stay on earth than he desired.

During these four years he had felt himself slowly being emptied. Emptied of pride, emptied of ambition. Emptied of anger, cunning, curiosity about the affairs of kings. Emptied of everything, except the desire to be one with God. The state of mind for which he had prayed all his life was given to him now. In his last days he became what his followers believed him to be, a holy man.

At the same time Columba was emptied of physical strength. The tall, sinewy man who had walked hundreds of miles over moors and mountains quietly dwindled. His thin body shrank, so that his habit hung like a sack on his frail bones. When he began to see the angels waiting on the rock again, he was glad. For him, these perfect summer days were God's last earthly gift.

On an afternoon towards the end of May, Columba said to Diarmaid, "Ask Feachtnach and Eochaidh to fetch a cart for me to sit in. I want to visit our brothers in the fields on the other side of the island."

It hurt Diarmaid to see Columba still pushing himself beyond the limits of his strength, praying on the seashore in the middle of the night, copying the psalter when he was barely able to hold his pen. He longed to say, "Father, you're not up to this any more. Let me put down some sheepskins in your cell, and make you comfortable in a decent bed." But Columba was his abbot, and his duty was to obey. So he said, "Yes, father," and went to tell Feachtnach to bring the cart. "Put lots of straw in it, and a fleece," he said anxiously. "Otherwise he'll be shaken to pieces. His bones are like dry twigs."

Feachtnach and Eochaidh harnessed a placid grey pony and backed it into the shafts of a small cart. Diarmaid helped the old man in, and they set off, Eochaidh leading the pony, Diarmaid and Feachtnach walking on either side. It was a pearly day, so still that you could hear bees humming and crickets shrilling above the background music of the sea. The cart carried Columba along tracks beaten by sandalled feet, to the fields where brothers were reaping barley that ought not, by nature's pattern, to have ripened until August. They dropped their reaping-hooks as the cart approached, and gathered round.

To Diarmaid's disapproval, Columba insisted on getting out of the cart and standing on a little hill. He could feel alone these days, even when he was surrounded by people, and he spent a few minutes in the isolation of silence, looking his last on the great green ocean, thinking of Erin, beyond the rim of the sky. Then he turned, and looked into the upturned faces of his monks.

"My dear sons," he said. "A month ago, at Easter, I wanted to leave this life, and be with God. But I didn't want that happy festival to become a sad time for you, so I decided to wait a little longer before asking God to take me home. Now, the time is near. I know that after today you will never see my face anywhere in this field."

Of course the brothers had known for ages that this parting was coming. But somehow, as long as it wasn't actually mentioned they had managed to hope that it might yet be deferred. Hearing it spelt out finally took that hope away, and many could not hold back their tears. Columba had always been there—sometimes harsh, sometimes kind, but always confident, resourceful, and strong. They did not know how they could live without him.

Columba tried to comfort them, but he knew that they must find their own way through grief and insecurity. He was tired. He could wait no longer. Turning to the east, he held up his thin old hands and blessed Í.

"From this moment," he said, "poisonous reptiles shall not be able to hurt either people or cattle on this island, so long as the inhabitants keep the commandments of Christ."

Then, with Diarmaid's help, he got back into the cart, and went home.

During the following ten days Columba again saw angels, and felt even more detached from the life he was about to leave. He was not afraid. On the Saturday that ended the first week of June, he again called Diarmaid to him. "I want to walk over to the barn," he said. "Let me lean on you."

Obediently Diarmaid offered his arm, and they set out, walking slowly across the ráth in the sunshine and along a little path to the thatched wooden building where the corn was stored. Inside it was cool and dark, but by the faint light that filtered through the air-vents high up on the walls, Columba could see two substantial heaps of winnowed corn lying on the floor.

"That's good," he said. "Our brothers are to be congratulated. I'm glad to know that, when I leave you, you will have enough bread for the year."

As always when Columba used the word "leave," a cold finger touched Diarmaid's heart. Deeply unhappy, he peered at the old man through he dim, dusty air of the barn. "Oh, father," he whispered. "Please, don't. Do you know how much you're vexing us with all this talk of leaving?"

Columba sighed, and took Diarmaid's hands in his. Thirty-four years they had been together, since that first crossing from Derry to Í. Diarmaid had been only fifteen. With his last intense feeling of human love, Columba realised how sore and forlorn Diarmaid was.

"My dear son," he said, "I have a little secret to tell you, if you'll promise not to tell anyone until after my death."

He knew how much it would mean to Diarmaid afterwards to have had his master's confidence. Diarmaid sank onto his knees. "I promise," he said hoarsely.

"In the Bible," Columba said, "Saturday is called

the sabbath, the day of rest. This is Saturday, and it really is a sabbath for me, for it is the last day of my life on earth. Tonight, at midnight, before the Lord's Day begins, I shall go into Paradise. Christ has invited me, Diarmaid," he went on, as Diarmaid began to sob bitterly. "I must go at his invitation. Try not to weep, my son. Wait patiently, for he will invite you, too."

Somehow, poor Diarmaid choked back the flood of tears that longed to be shed, and they set off, back in the direction of the monastery. Half way, Columba was tired.

"Sit down for a little, father," said Diarmaid.

"I think I will," Columba replied.

Diarmaid gently lowered the old man onto a stone that stood by the side of the path, and himself sat down on the grass beside him. They had only been there for a few moments when they heard a clopping of hooves over the hard, sandy turf.

"Here's an old friend," Columba said.

Indeed it was. The old white horse that for years had carried the milk pails from the cowshed to the monastery, but was now put out to grass, had seen Columba, and come to greet him. Many a kind word the horse had had from the abbot, and many tasty morsels from his hand. Now it knelt down and, as if understanding the old man's frailty, lightly placed its muzzle against his chest.

Then a very strange thing happened. The horse began to weep. Cries of distress broke from its foaming mouth, while tears like a human being's poured from its eyes, wetting Columba's habit. Deeply moved, Columba patted the creature's head, and made soothing noises, which it seemed to understand.

Unhappiness made Diarmaid irritable. "We can't have this!" he snapped. "Shoo, horse! Go away!"

But Columba shook his head. "Leave it alone, Diarmaid," he said. "You know about my departure, because I've just told you. But doesn't it seem wonderful to you that this horse knows too? God himself must have told it that its master is about to leave it."

Then Columba blessed the horse. Sadly, it rose from its knees and wandered away.

On the way back, Columba made a little detour. From a mound above the monastery he blessed it and all the people who would in the future come to the island for his sake. Then he returned to his cell, not to rest but to go on with his daily stint of copying the scriptures. He was working on the thirty-fourth psalm. He wrote steadily for a while, but when he got to the verse that says, *They that seek the Lord shall not want any good thing*, he put down his pen. It seemed a perfect place to stop.

"I think I can write no more," he said.

During the evening, livid clouds massed over the mountains of Mull. Towards sunset they unfurled like ragged grey flags, effacing the luminous twilight of the northern summer night. Sea and sky darkened, and in the stillness that sometimes precedes a storm, lightning flickered eerily.

Diarmaid saw it through chinks in the walls of the cell where he sat waiting, while Columba rested on his stony bed. Since childhood, Diarmaid had been terrified of storms, but now he felt nothing. His grief had drained him, and he really didn't care what happened to him any more. From time to time he glanced over his shoulder at the still figure, dimly visible on the floor. It was impossible to say whether Columba woke or slept. Anyway, Diarmaid's business was to wait. The last minutes of his waiting passed leadenly. Soon it would be all over.

Just before midnight Scannal rang the monastery bell. Its clear, solemn voice warned the brothers that it was time for midnight service in the church. The tiny lamps that they carried began to appear like fireflies at the doors of their cells, and Diarmaid, when he had lit his, turned to help Columba to rise. To his astonishment, he saw there was no need.

Columba was already on his feet. He was smiling. Without a word he brushed past Diarmaid, and, with a last, miraculous return of his old strength, ran in the darkness across the grass to the church. He reached the threshold first, exultant, as if he were running a race.

Now Columba could see his goal. Throwing open the door, he hurried through the church. For a glorious moment he was alive, his heart filled with a happiness that was airy and leafy and bright with the promise of youthful days, when all good things are still to come. Joyfully, he fell on his knees before the altar.

Diarmaid arrived just ahead of the other monks. For a second he saw the church lit up in a blinding burst of white light, which seemed to come from the head of the kneeling man. Then it was dark. The sudden contrast confused Diarmaid.

"Father, where are you?" he cried, groping fearfully towards the altar.

It was Feachtnach who answered. "It's all right, Diarmaid. Hold on. We're here."

The other brothers came with their lamps. In the new, subdued light, Diarmaid found his way to his master, who was now lying across the altar steps. Kneeling down, Diarmaid raised Columba in his arms, supporting the drooping head against his shoulder. "I'm here, father," he whispered.

The brothers gathered round, their eyes large and dark in the flickering lamplight. Some of them sobbed, but others gazed in awe at the radiant face of Columba. All the lines of age and pain had been smoothed away and his youth renewed. Diarmaid took Columba's right arm by the wrist and raised it up. "Give us your blessing, father," he begged.

Columba was beyond speech, but he managed to lift his hand and make the sign of the Cross. Minutes later, he stopped breathing.

One day long before, when they were walking together on the shore, Diarmaid had said to Columba, "You know, father, when you die, all the people in Dál Riada will row across to your funeral. I really don't know how we'll be able to accommodate them."

Then he had blushed at his own tactlessness.

But Columba had merely given him an amused look, and replied in his usual confident, prophetic way, "No, my son. It won't turn out that way. No-one will be able to come to my funeral, and I shall be buried as I wish, privately, by my own monks."

And of course, he was right.

In the hours that followed Columba's death, the wind rose. First it wailed, then it screamed, and in the grey, cheerless dawn of Sunday the weary brothers saw the water of the sound thrashing and boiling in fury. Huge, foam-crested waves thundered onto the shore. For three days and nights a rainless tempest howled round Í, preventing even the most intrepid sailor from putting to sea.

The brothers who had known and loved Columba wrapped his body in fine linen. While the storm raged they took it in turn to watch and pray beside him. On the fourth day they buried him, with many tears. His funeral was, as he wished, a family affair.

For many years after his death, stories about Columba were spread, in the tradition of his people, by word of mouth. No doubt many of them became more colourful in the telling. After about seventy years a little book about Columba's good deeds was written by Cuimín the Fair, who was the seventh abbot of Í. But not until a century had passed were all the stories collected and written down in Adhamhnán's *Life of St Columba*. Adhamhnán, like Columba, was of the family of Conall Gulban. He became abbot of Í in the year 679.

By that date Í had another name. Adhamhnán, who wrote in Latin, called it "Ioua insula," which probably means island with yews. It seems that by a mistake in copying it the word "Ioua" became altered to "Iona," which is the name of Columba's island today. By an odd but happy coincidence, Iona is the Latin form of the Hebrew name Jonah. Jonah in Hebrew, like Colm in Irish and Columba in Latin, means "dove."

Ceanntiarna is known in Scotland as Kentigern, or Mungo, who is the patron saint of Glasgow (Glaschù). His teacher, Searbhán, is called Servanus, or Serf.

Children's
POOLBEG

To get regular
information about
our books and authors join

THE POOLBEG
BOOK CLUB

To become a member of
THE POOLBEG BOOK CLUB
Write to Anne O'Reilly,
The Poolbeg Book Club,
Knocksedan House,
Swords, Co. Dublin.
Please write clearly and make sure to include
all the following details: Name, full address,
date of birth, school.